PARENT

VS.

PARENT

PARENT vs. PARENT

*How You and Your Child
Can Survive
the Custody Battle*

PARENT

STEPHEN P. HERMAN, M.D.

PANTHEON BOOKS NEW YORK

Grateful acknowledgment is made to John Wiley & Sons,
Inc., for permission to reprint an excerpt from Interventions for Children of Divorce by William F. Hodges.
Copyright © 1986 by John Wiley & Sons, Inc. Reprinted
by permission of John Wiley & Sons, Inc.

Library of Congress Cataloging-in-Publication Data

Herman, Stephen P., 1946–
Parent vs. parent: how you and your child can survive the
custody battle/Stephen P. Herman.
p. cm.
Includes bibliographical references.
ISBN 0-394-57173-8
1. Custody of children—United States—Popular works.
2. Divorce suits—United States—Popular works.
3. Custody of children—United States—
Psychological aspects.
I. Title.
KF547.Z9H47 1990
346.7301'7—dc20
[347.30617]   89-43256

Book Design by Guenet Abraham

MANUFACTURED IN THE UNITED STATES OF AMERICA
FIRST EDITION

To Joan

C O N T E N T S

Acknowledgments ix

Introduction 3

1. *Divorce, Custody, and the Family 7*

2. *Whose Child Is It, Anyway? 24*

3. *Mediation 46*

4. *Think Before You Act 61*

5. *Telling the Children 79*

6. *Building Your Case 91*

7. *The Expert Witness 106*

8. *Some Special Issues 122*

9. *Your Day in Court 147*

10. *The Decision 162*

11. *Visitation 176*

12. *Relitigation 194*

13. *Does Your Child Need Therapy? 203*

14. *Conclusion: Is There Life After a Custody Dispute? 221*

Appendix 229

Notes 233

Index 237

ACKNOWLEDGMENTS

MANY PEOPLE HAVE contributed directly and indirectly to the preparation of this book.

In my medical training, I have been fortunate in having had outstanding teachers—at the Mayo Clinic, in Rochester, Minnesota: Drs. Gunnar Stickler, Gerald Gilchrist, and Alexander Lucas; at Montefiore Medical Center, in New York City: Drs. Robert Schulman, Bennett Rosner, and John Jacobs; and at the Yale Child Study Center, in New Haven, Connecticut: Drs. Albert Solnit, John Schowalter, Melvin Lewis, and Donald Cohen, and also Barbara Nordhaus, M.S.W.

My colleagues in child psychiatry and psychology have both instructed and inspired me: in Rockport, Maine, Dr. Diane Schetky, one of the founders of the field of forensic child psychiatry and my mentor, most generous chief booster, and close friend; in New York City, Drs. Alan Levy, Alex Weintrob, Theodore Shapiro, Lee Salk, and Angel Martinez.

Lawyers who work so hard for children and their families, and whose ethics exemplify the best of the legal profession, have taught me much: Eleanor Alter, Helene Brezinski, James Abramson, and Benjamin Rosin.

Those who believed in this book from the beginning and gave of their time and expertise have helped bring it to fruition: Judith Appelbaum and Florence Janovic of Sensible Solutions, in New York City; editor Sara Blackburn; at Pantheon, my editor, Sara Bershtel, Julie Phillips, Jeannine Ciliotta, and Ann Martin; and typist Rachel Burd.

I am also grateful for the love and support of my family: my father, Hyman Herman, Esq., trial attorney for over four decades, a most honest and selfless man; my mother, Ruth Herman, schoolteacher and amateur psychologist (who's usually right about everything); my sister, Beth Herman, R.N., who has always put up with too much from her older brother; and Joan Grant Herman, my wife and the love of my life, actress, partner, and best friend, who endured clacking computer keys, jammed printers, and power surges, and who somehow knew this book would finally get written when I had all but given up.

Finally, to the many parents and children, those in crisis and those who have found some peace and equanimity: thank you for letting me into your lives, for trusting me with your most personal struggles, and for teaching me so much.

PARENT

vs.

PARENT

INTRODUCTION

CHILDREN GROWING UP in the United States today have about an even chance of living in a household with both biological parents or living in a household broken by divorce. When their parents separate or divorce, almost all children develop some symptoms of psychological distress. These are usually magnified by a custody battle. Unfortunately, most parents have no idea of the psychological impact of a custody dispute on their children. They are often completely caught up in their own feelings—or they succumb to the temptation of wanting to believe that the children are just fine. They tell their friends, "They're handling it very well." Plenty of people will offer advice—and even strategies to wrest the child away from the "evil" ex-partner—to parents battling for custody; among them will probably be friends, neighbors, and anyone who has gone through a custody battle. But few indeed will regard the children as the center of the process or as its potential victims.

A custody dispute is a seriously flawed procedure for deciding where and how children will live. Even the terms used to describe it are unfortunate: "custody" implies ownership and perpetuates the ancient view of children as property. And a custody "battle" can hardly be in the best interests of the children. Some clinicians, such as Dr. Lee Salk of The New York Hospital-Cornell Medical Center, avoid such expressions altogether. Dr. Salk prefers to talk with parents and judges not about custody, but about which parent should have "primary responsibility" for the child. But even though an approach such as Dr. Salk's may help mitigate the tension, anxiety, and conflict surrounding child custody cases, most custody decisions do enter the adversarial system, do turn into battles, and do get out of control.

This book will prepare you for what to expect, both psychologically and factually, for yourself and your child if you become involved in the complex business of custody proceedings. It is certainly not a guide to "winning" a custody battle, and it is not intended to take the place of the work and advice of competent lawyers or child behavior experts. But it will broaden your perspective and help you to become as child-centered as possible, so that you can actively work to limit the harm to your child or children.

Part I (chapters 1–4) presents an overview of the relevant areas of psychiatry and the law and reviews the history of child placement conflicts. It describes how these disputes have been handled by the courts over the years, as well as the various alternatives to full-blown custody battles, such as mediation or joint custody. You will be able to assess the pros and cons of these alternatives in order to have some perspective on their appropriateness for your family. As you'll discover, much depends upon the personalities of the parents and the children, and upon the adults' success (or lack thereof) in being able to view the divorce and the custody decision as a problem to be solved rather than as a bargaining chip in a power struggle that only one side can win.

Part II (chapters 5–9) takes you step by step through the events leading up to your day in court. These chapters prepare you for the shock of having to involve a series of strangers—lawyers, court-appointed experts—in your private family affairs, and show you how to use their services to best advantage. You will also learn what to expect from the actual courtroom experience—and what not to expect.

Part III focuses on the impact of the custody decision on you and your children—and its aftermath. It covers such topics as visitation and relitigation and discusses how to decide whether your child needs psychological treatment. The ·final chapter deals with some of the long-term effects of custody disputes on the family.

What you learn may surprise you, but it should also enable you to help your children during what is sure to be a most stressful period in their lives. As a child psychiatrist and a frequent court-appointed expert in custody suits, I have become very aware of a family's need for guidance before or during this most difficult time—not after the fact, when otherwise avoidable damage may have been done. Certainly it would be best to avoid a custody dispute altogether, for I do not believe such a dispute ever solves many problems. It may lead to a decision about where a child is placed, but getting to that decision involves such anguish that the victory is strictly a Pyrrhic one.

I've presented clinical examples of parents and children caught up in these disputes to illustrate what others have gone through and the choices they have made. Though names and details have been changed to protect confidentiality, the cases are drawn from actual professional experience. The occasional criticisms of lawyers are made from the point of view of the psychological needs of the child, not from the perspective of the "correct" legal strategy to achieve a "victory." I work with many sensitive and caring lawyers in my practice. And in fairness, I have not hesitated to be critical of the judiciary and of my own colleagues when criticism is warranted.

In an ideal world—one free of marital strife and children's unhappiness—this book would not have to be written. But as long as divorce continues to be so common and our society so inclined to lawsuits, we will continue to be confronted with child custody disputes, and we will need to deal with the toll they take on all the participants. My aim here has been to provide as informative and complete a treatment of the topics and issues as possible. My hope is that this book will help you make careful and informed choices in a difficult situation and provide you with the understanding and confidence to move ahead with your life and to safeguard your children's future.

DIVORCE, CUSTODY, AND THE FAMILY

IT NO LONGER comes as a surprise that divorce is common in the United States. While there is some indication that the figure is decreasing, nearly 50 percent of marriages now end in divorce. If we have not been divorced ourselves, almost all of us know people who have, and our children know other children who have lived through their parents' divorce.

Each year, divorce affects about a million children. And a full 10 percent of all divorces involving children end in litigated custody proceedings, placing thousands of children in the middle of protracted legal disputes.[1]

These figures all point to a dramatic departure from the romanticized view of the family: mother, father, and children living happily together in a stable unit bound by biology and love. That image has been eroding rapidly; indeed, today more children live in step- or single-parent families than in nuclear families. Whether or not there will be a swing back to the more traditional model remains to be seen. But for the immediate future, a substantial number of children and their parents will continue to face the kinds of problems brought on by divorce and custody disputes.

Let's take a fairly typical example. Ten-year-old Peter Carson was in psychotherapy with Dr. James Harrison because of a moderate depression brought on by learning disabilities, failure at school, and his parents' unhappy marriage. Dr. Harrison was especially concerned when Peter began to come late to sessions and then one day announced he did not want to continue. He said the time he spent with Dr. Harrison was a waste and their sessions together only made him sad. Peter's schoolwork had deteriorated still further by this time, and he was also having great difficulty getting along with his peers at school and in the neighborhood.

Dr. Harrison finally learned from the father that Peter's parents were getting a divorce. Mr. Carson had broken the news to his son gently. He told Peter that he and Peter's mother were no longer able to live together, although they both loved Peter very much. He said that he wasn't sure where they all would live, but that one thing was certain: both his mother and his father would remain very close to Peter and would still be very much involved in his life.

Unfortunately, Mrs. Carson had been less diplomatic. She told her son that his father had a serious alcohol problem and also that he had been involved with other women. She said that on many occasions he had come home drunk, boasting about his love affairs and daring his wife to do something about them.

She even told Peter that his father had twice struck her across the face.

After speaking with both parents, Dr. Harrison asked Peter if anything happening in the family might be upsetting him. Peter became angry and denied that there were problems at home. Then he began to cry.

"My parents are getting a divorce," he finally blurted out.

After he calmed down, Dr. Harrison asked him if he knew what a divorce meant.

"Sure I do," said Peter. "Tommy's parents got divorced and so did Susan Fielding's. It's going to be totally different now. We're not going to be a family any more. I never thought this would happen in our house. My father doesn't drink! He never got drunk. My mother is a liar!"

"How will it be different?" Dr. Harrison asked.

"Me and my father are gonna get kicked out of the house. Maybe my mother will let us live out in the backyard, I'm not sure. We'll probably have to live in a tent, though. It won't be very big. I hope we can both fit in it. We won't have much to eat any more, either. Maybe a can of tuna fish, I don't know."

Peter started to cry again. Later in the session, he told Dr. Harrison about an experience he had had a year earlier. A carnival had come to town, and many children were lining up for the rides. The most popular was a spinning wheel, which held screaming children along its outer rim. It would spin faster and faster, tilting as it spun. Peter had waited in line, hoping to get on the ride with several other children from his class. Unfortunately, the operator of the ride cut the line just ahead of Peter, and he had to wait until the next cycle. By the time it was his turn, his friends had gone on to another attraction, and Peter had the dubious distinction of being the only child on the ride. As the wheel began to spin, he realized people on the ground were watching him. He felt silly, because he was sure everyone was staring and laughing at him. Although the other boys and girls had seemed to have a wonderful time on the ride, Peter hated every minute of it. All he had wanted was to be one of the group, enjoying himself with his classmates. Instead, he felt like an outcast.

Peter didn't know why he remembered this incident on that particular day. Dr. Harrison suggested that his memory of the ride was connected to the present problem of his parents' divorce. In fact, Dr. Harrison went on, Peter might even be feeling now just the way he did when all those people seemed to be staring at him on the ride: as if he were somehow different from the others, alone and isolated. Dr. Harrison told Peter that many children felt just the way he did. He said he hoped Peter and he would continue to talk so that Peter could start to understand how his own life could go on even as his parents embarked on new lives apart from each other.

IF YOU ARE like most divorcing parents, you are very much concerned about the welfare of your children even in the middle of your own personal turmoil. You would like to believe that they will emerge from this period of great stress without too much suffering and without any scars. If you are contemplating a custody dispute or are already involved in one, you probably hope your children realize you are doing this for their own good and will somehow and someday understand your decision. Unfortunately, virtually all children seem to develop some behavioral problems during a divorce. And children of all ages who must also deal with a custody battle have an especially difficult time.

□ THE DIFFICULT PATH □

Divorce is, of course, hard on everyone, but it is especially hard on couples with children. A couple without children has a much greater chance of ending an unsuccessful marriage with a minimum of psychological distress. Such a couple may feel some embarrassment and shame, and a sense of having failed. If the divorce was not mutually agreed upon, one spouse may feel deeply hurt and disappointed, and might be at increased risk for depression. After the divorce, neither may be willing to become involved in another relationship for a while. However, most people without children are eventually able to bounce back to a happier and more fulfilling life, and are likely to remarry.

For couples with children, however, the stakes are much higher. Divorcing parents grieve not only for themselves, but also for their children, whom they feel they have let down. Divorce thus becomes the equivalent of an intense mourning process. For women, feelings can include extreme disappointment with the spouse, embarrassment and humiliation, fear of economic devastation or instability, loneliness, and guilt. A woman who retains custody—and 89 percent of women do—often regards her ex-husband as irresponsible. She may be dissatisfied with his seeming lack of involvement with the children and angry about the amount of child support she receives. Some women may wonder if they will ever be able to meet a new man now that they are "saddled" with the children. Of all these fears, those relating to economic instability are probably the most realistic, for most women with children do indeed suffer financially after divorce. Conversely, the divorced father's income often rises significantly.

Yet, it would be naïve to think that husbands do not react as emotionally to divorce as wives do. They also seem to have a difficult time.[2] Men whose marriages have ended describe themselves as feeling lonely, at loose ends, and envious of those in fulfilling relationships. Although some men may turn to friends for solace, many often withdraw from social contacts. While it is true that some men do feel immense relief at being "free" of their wives and the burdens of parenthood, most suffer after the marital breakup. Divorced men, for example, are nine times more likely to be admitted to psychiatric hospitals for the first time than are men in successful marriages.

In addition, divorced fathers who no longer live with their children often have a hard time adjusting to the idea of visitation. Those who spend more satisfying, happy times with their children after a divorce than they did during the marriage are often less depressed than those who cannot enjoy seeing their children on a schedule. Those who have arrived at successful joint custody arrangements with their ex-wives and who have frequent, unimpeded visits with their children seem to do best.

Adjustment to divorce is just as difficult for children as it is for adults. Many children, like Peter Carson, may develop special fears about the future; they may become convinced that terrible things are going to happen to them. All children, no matter how secure they feel or how amicable their parents' divorce, must overcome a series of challenges—or obstacles—in order to reestablish some sort of psychological equilibrium. Researcher Judith Wallerstein has identified the tasks facing these children as (1) acknowledging the reality of the divorce, (2) disengaging from parental conflicts to renew their own interests, (3) resolving their sense of loss, (4) resolving anger and self-blame, (5) accepting the permanence of the divorce, and (6) achieving realistic hope for their own future relationships.[3] Wallerstein notes that a child's ability to negotiate these obstacles depends upon three factors: the age and developmental level of the child, the child's temperament or personality, and his or her previous life experiences and family interactions. Let us review the six tasks confronting children of divorce.

The first task is simply to acknowledge the reality of the separation. Human beings of all ages have an uncanny—and often powerful—ability to defend themselves against having to deal with painful experiences. Psychiatrists call this defense mechanism "denial." The shock of learning about their parents' separation and divorce may lead children to deny the seriousness of these events, or even their very existence. A child may minimize the degree of his feelings, or insist that nothing bad is happening. He may be able to admit that his parents fight—even that they yell at each other a lot—but he may refuse to accept the fact that they will no longer live together. He may try to use fantasies in an attempt to undo or reverse what has happened. Even after one parent has already moved out, some children will still talk about their family as if both parents are at home and all is well. Some children in denial will need help from a therapist; others are able to overcome their shock and confusion with the aid of the immediate family and other adults, such as teachers or neighbors. Sometimes other children, especially those who have themselves gone through divorce, can help particularly resistant children to begin to accept the truth.

Younger children—who typically believe that the world revolves around them—often have trouble disengaging themselves from their parents' conflict. When they first learn about an impending separation and divorce, they often feel that they themselves have the power to fix things and make them right. In addition, they may believe the divorce is happening because of them, and that therefore they must stop it.

Jodie was nine when her parents began divorce proceedings. Although her mother and father were living apart, they had been unable to begin the process of separating emotionally from each other, and Jodie heard them arguing constantly. She was living with her mother, and whenever her father called the house and she heard the inevitable yelling begin, Jodie would pick up the telephone herself and scream and beg them to stop fighting. On most occasions, of course, she would be unsuccessful and would run crying to her room. It was not surprising that Jodie was unable to separate herself from this conflict, for her parents' ongoing, angry enmeshment prevented them from helping her to do so. Each knew that Jodie felt responsible for the breakup and talked to Jodie many times about how the situation had nothing to do with her. But despite their pleas to her not to become involved in their arguments, Jodie persisted in her peacemaking role. She was having great difficulty with the task of disengagement.

Just like adults, children faced with the breakup of their family experience intense feelings of loss, which they must deal with and resolve. They undergo the loss of the family as they have known it, the loss of intimacy with one or both parents, and the loss of shared family routines and traditions. Some children tolerate and cope with these losses better than others, but most go through a lengthy mourning process as they begin to accept the separation and divorce. Profoundly saddened by the breakup, some children are unable to function as well as they once did. They may lose interest in play and become withdrawn, schoolwork may be affected, and peer relationships may suffer. Eventually, most children are able to stop grieving, but it may take them years to come to terms with the fact that life will never be the same again.

As children work through this mourning process, they may also experience feelings of humiliation and powerlessness—feelings that are also difficult for adults to overcome. (For some, the inability to deal with this sense of helplessness and powerlessness may lead to depression years later.) And there are often feelings of anger and self-blame to overcome as well.

When Peter, the ten-year-old we described earlier, first learned of his parents' impending divorce, he became angry. However, his anger was directed in a very selective way. Once he realized he would probably be living with his mother, he became very angry at her: he accused her of turning his father out of the house and of ruining the family's happiness. He began to throw things around the house, something he had never done before.

Younger children, who lack the cognitive skills to make sense of the complicated feelings surrounding divorce, often fix blame on one or both parents, or on themselves. This makes events more understandable to them, but ascribing blame can lead to anger. The anger, in turn, can take two main forms: "acting out" or "acting in." When children act out, they may become unusually aggressive at school—hitting other children, calling them names, refusing to share, speaking out of turn. They may also become hyperactive, unable to sit still or pay attention to anything for very long. When children act in, they turn their feelings inward, and develop symptoms we call "psychosomatic." They may become withdrawn or moody, and complain of headaches, "tummyaches," or other nonspecific problems. They may also become generally fearful, suffer sleep disturbances, or develop eating problems. Most children of divorcing parents experience a combination of both reactions.

Eventually, almost all children learn to forgive their parents as well as themselves for the marital breakup, but the process may take years. It is vital for parents to recognize that this particular task—forgiveness—can be extremely difficult for children. Divorcing parents must resist the temptation to believe that talking candidly and lovingly to their children will prevent—or quickly heal—the sense of loss. There is just so much that even the most loving parent can do in this situation. Some suffering is inevitable, given the dimensions of the change and the loss.

Children can begin to accept the permanence of their parents' divorce only when they are well on their way toward resolving the other tasks, for this long-range acceptance is perhaps the most difficult challenge of all. Some children hold tenaciously to the hope that their parents will reconcile. They may be encouraged in this by knowing that their mother and father are in some sort of counseling, and may persist in the fantasy even when they are told that the counseling is divorce mediation. Children may then pin their hopes on the counselor as a potential reconciler. Young children who have heard that their parents are going to court may believe that the judge will somehow make them love each other again and bring them back together to live an idyllic family life.

In some ways, accepting the divorce as permanent may be even more difficult for children than coming to terms with the actual death of a parent, for although the family has indeed "died," each parent is still alive, apparently available to bring the "dead" family back to life. The child's love for both parents may be very strong, and she may be unable to accept that the parents cannot love each other equally strongly. Only with support and understanding, as well as the maturity that normal development brings, can the child come to recognize the finality of the divorce and get on with life.

And this, perhaps, is the most important task for the child of divorce to master: to overcome the hurt and disappointment and to look toward the future with hope and optimism. As they enter adolescence, children begin to form relationships of intimacy and commitment. It is important for them to approach this stage of their lives with the ability to separate their own fate from that of their parents. They can only do this if they have successfully completed the previous tasks and developed a healthy sense of self.

□ DIFFERENT AGES, □ DIFFERENT FEELINGS

Children from birth to about two years of age will certainly not have a cognitive understanding of their parents' separation. However, even infants are acutely aware of tension and anxiety. And certainly if the primary caregiver leaves, the child will be aware of the change and will have some reaction. In most cases, as we have said, it is the mother who retains custody of the child, at least at the beginning of the separation. She may very well be upset by the changes in her life, and an infant will most likely sense this upset. Some very young children develop eating or sleeping problems. They may display digestive symptoms, such as diarrhea, constipation, or abdominal pain. They may cry more often and be less easily consoled. Sometimes, when parental separation brings with it a sudden change of place, the young child faced with unfamiliar surroundings, smells, or sounds will become fearful and agitated.

Children of two or three, just at the age when they are beginning to explore their world and separate a bit from their parents, may be impeded in this important developmental stage if a major change threatens their sense of security. Whether they experience the loss of the noncustodial parent or the distress of the custodial parent, children of this age may well become frightened and saddened by what is happening. They may express their feelings by regressing: if they have been toilet-trained, for example, they may revert to soiling themselves and wetting the bed. They may have severe temper tantrums, become more dependent on certain objects, such as a blanket or stuffed animal, or demonstrate signs of increased anxiety, such as head-banging, compulsive rocking, or constant masturbation. Such children may do better if their parents explain what has happened and what is likely to happen, and reassure them that they will not be abandoned. Even at this age, children need to know what has happened to the absent parent and why he or she has left the home.

Children of three to five go through their own set of problems when they experience separation and divorce. The child may want to sleep in the same bed as the parent. The parent may be tempted to rationalize this by saying, "Oh, he needs me. It's just temporary. He won't sleep unless he's with me," but such a move should be discouraged. It can set up a mutual dependency that may be hard to break. Children of this age may also respond to a divorce with displays of pseudomaturity —a boy sometimes "protecting" his mother, for example, or a girl acting as if she were grown-up. (A daughter, for instance, may try to comfort her mother by saying, "You'll be all right, Mommy. Don't cry. I can make lunch for us and I'll help clean up the house.) Such behavior is usually intended to cover up fear and anxiety, and should also be gently discouraged. Children at this stage may be so anxious that they may not wish to further rock the boat by expressing their own feelings or by complaining. They may appear to be very good and cooperative, leading parents to assume, quite erroneously, that everything is just fine.

Children of five and six may also demonstrate increased depression, irritability, moodiness, and anxiety. They may have difficulty falling asleep and, again, want to stay in the parent's bedroom. They may have nightmares. Such children may not want to go to school, or they may develop new fears: of dogs, insects, or the dark.

By the time children are eight or nine, they will have considerably more understanding of the implications of the parental separation and at least an intellectual appreciation of the permanence of divorce. Although it is impossible to predict how children will react, some experts believe that when parents separate at this time in a child's life, the event may have a less negative impact than it would at another stage, partly because the child is more mature and may turn for support and solace to friends and teachers. What we do know, however, is that children at this age tend to take sides when faced with a separation. Placing the blame on one parent makes it easier for the child to make sense of a complicated and unhappy situation. Both parents, therefore, need to take special care to avoid pressuring a child to choose one parent with whom to identify and ally himself.

Children in the preteen years also have a tendency to take sides. Parents may be tempted to turn to preteen children as confidants and supportive friends. Sometimes the child is all too willing to listen to one parent's complaints about the other, and subtly—without even being aware of it—the parent may begin to seek the child's advice and guidance. Once this pattern is established, it can be very difficult to break. The result is often a child whose own anxiety is compounded by the pressure of having to be the parent's pal.

Twelve-year-old Sallie Richardson lived with her mother. Her parents had been divorced for about two years, and Sallie's father had been remarried, to a well-known actress. He and his new wife lived very well, while Sallie's mother had to struggle to make ends meet, in spite of regular child support payments from Mr. Richardson. The first Mrs. Richardson did not hesitate to let Sallie know at every available opportunity what she thought of her father. When Sallie was referred for psychotherapy after her grades fell without explanation, her mother told the psychiatrist that she and Sallie had "the perfect mother-daughter relationship. In fact," she continued, "we're not just mother and daughter; we're good friends. Sallie is my whole life. She understands me. She knows what a bastard her father really is. I don't have to tell her. She can see for herself. She's very bright, you know. Why should I try to hide it from her? I hate the man."

Sallie told the therapist: "I understand my mom. My dad sure doesn't. I'm the only one who can make her happy when she feels sad."

"Do you ever argue with her?" the therapist asked.

"Nope. We never argue. Maybe she'll get a little annoyed if I let my room get too messy. Besides that, we get along great. It's my dad that I fight with. He's a pain. He's a liar, too. And he never wants to see me. He's got his fancy new wife to be with. He doesn't have time for me any more. I don't care, though. Who wants to be with him? He's a jerk!"

At some point, Sallie will probably resent having been forced into the role of her mother's best friend. There's a good chance she'll become quite angry with her mother, and at that point their "perfect relationship" may suddenly end. Meanwhile, behaving like her mother's peer was taking a toll, interfering with her concentration in school and preventing her from acting her age.

Adolescents also have a difficult time with separation and divorce. The fact that they are older and can understand more does not mean they do not suffer pain and loss. They are already grappling with a number of important development issues, such as identity, sexuality, and emotional separation from the family, so coping with family conflict only adds to their stresses. Adolescents already in the process of trying to separate from the family may increase their efforts at this time, staying away from home as much as possible and seeking solace with friends. Many young people may be tempted to experiment with illicit drugs and alcohol or be sexually promiscuous. Such behaviors may actually mask serious depression.

Other adolescents may withdraw. As their self-esteem plummets, they may feel less inclined to go out with friends, to date, to attend school, or to participate in social activities. They prefer to remain alone, watching television or listening to records and tapes. They may overeat, or they may hardly eat at all.

Adolescents are most likely to do better if both parents remain involved in their lives and make special efforts not to engage them in grown-up battles. The higher the childrens' self-esteem before the separation and the more outside interests and support they have, the easier their adjustment will be.

Researchers have noted that children of all ages continue to react to the parental breakup for years afterward. As Dr. William Hodges puts it in *Interventions for Children of Divorce,* a manual for mental health clinicians and legal experts:

> Particularly for preschool and early school age children, there is reason to believe that a significant number will be seen as worse off for the next one to two years. For older children, the adjustment level may not deteriorate, but improvement may not occur.[4]

Within a few months to a year after the separation, children may appear to be doing better. Sleep disturbances may lessen, the mood may brighten, and schoolwork and peer relations may return to preseparation levels. Of course, a great deal depends on the emotional climate at home, the level of cooperation of the divorcing parents, economic considerations, and so on. Still, even in the best of postdivorce families, children report negative feelings and psychological pain for as long as ten years after the breakup. This does not suggest that children will be in psychological turmoil forever because of a divorce. What it does mean is that divorce has a profound and probably lifelong impact on children. And the more their parents continue to fight or to engage in prolonged legal proceedings, the more the children's development will suffer.

□ THE ADDED BURDEN OF □
A CUSTODY DISPUTE

In addition to the disappointment, anger, and frustration that accompany separation and divorce, children must bear an extra burden if their parents engage in a custody battle—and a battle it surely is if it has extended beyond the agreement to divorce.

All the problems described above will most likely be exacerbated. Certainly children of different ages and temperaments will respond differently. But they will all, unfortunately, face unhappy feelings and react in negative ways. If you are considering custody litigation, or have already been brought into it by the other parent, you will need to be aware of the kinds of problems it can cause for you and your children.

Benjamin Pearsall, seven, turned his emotions inward during his parents' separation and the subsequent custody battle. His personality changed dramatically. From being a lively, playful, and curious boy, he became withdrawn, sullen, and uninterested in playing with friends or in being with either parent. In his first-grade classroom, he no longer volunteered when the teacher asked for help, and he showed little or no motivation for schoolwork.

The most serious manifestation of his anxiety was compulsive eating. Benjy snacked continually, gorging on cookies, potato chips, ice cream, whatever was around the house. He also began to go from table to table in the school cafeteria, asking other children to give him their desserts. In two months, he gained fifteen pounds.

The problem was compounded by his parents' conflicting views of his eating behavior. Benjy's father was appalled by his son's weight gain and blamed the mother. He told the psychiatrist doing the court-ordered custody evaluation (discussed in chapter 7) that she indulged her son's every whim, encouraged him to drink two to three glasses of milk every day, allowed him daily ice cream and cookies, and so on. He took Benjy to a series of pediatricians to document that he was overweight. The father planned to use letters from these doctors when the custody dispute came to trial. He also insisted that Benjy engage in constant physical exercise with him on the weekends they spent together: he forced the child to jog, play softball and football, and do calisthenics.

Mrs. Pearsall, on the other hand, minimized Benjy's weight gain. She told him he looked fine the way he was and that his father was making a big thing out of nothing. She also took

Benjy to a doctor, who said the boy was fine and that because both parents were tall, he would thin out as he got older. Naturally, Mrs. Pearsall was gratified by this pronouncement. Benjy, on the other hand, was confused and seemed even more anxious than before. He continued to overeat.

Not all children, of course, develop overt signs of distress. Some become quietly sad. Others, though, make no secret of their feelings about the custody contest and their anger with one or both parents. This was certainly the case with Kristin Surrey and her family.

Most custody conflicts involve young children; the Surrey case was somewhat unusual in that it involved a fourteen-year-old girl. After announcing their intention to get a divorce and to engage in a custody dispute, both of Kristin's parents had continued to live in the same house. Kristin was absolutely furious about her parents' battle over her and made it clear to both of them that she was extremely upset by their constant fighting. She also told her father repeatedly that she wished to live with her mother and hoped that he would drop the case. She was verbally abusive to him on many occasions.

When Kristin and her father came for a joint session to the office of the therapist evaluating the family for the court, Kristin asked to sit as far away from her father as possible. She said to the therapist, "I just can't stand him. Why doesn't he leave me alone?" The father maintained a wan smile throughout the session and said he expected that his daughter would "come around" to his way of thinking after the litigation was over. But Kristin was deeply hurt, and it would take her a long time to get over her anger. In their own ways, both Kristin and Benjy were acting out the trauma and unhappiness of being drawn into their parents' tug-of-war.

This is a hard time for everyone. Like you, your children will be frustrated by the situation. Just as your emotions will take many turns, so will theirs. The potential for lasting damage is very real, and some of the hurt is simply unavoidable. What you can do is be available to them, and be sensitive and open to what they are going through. What follows is intended to help you learn how best to survive this difficult time: how to deal with the practical, legal, and psychological issues you will face, and how to minimize as much as possible the unhappiness of everyone involved.

WHOSE CHILD IS
IT, ANYWAY?

W H A T I S A custody dispute? When parents with children divorce, one of the most important issues for each of them becomes the fate of their children. As psychological extensions of themselves, as the symbol of their own hopes and dreams, children are inextricably linked with the parents' own sense of self. During divorce, a parent seeks to "save" himself or herself and the children as well. Emotions run high. A custody dispute represents the failure of the parents to work out an agreement on who will raise the children. A custody dispute, aptly called a custody "battle," will end either in a mediated settlement or in litigation. In mediation (discussed in chapter 3), both parents participate in reaching a settlement outside the court. In litigation, the parents use the adversarial system, hire their own lawyers, sometimes provide for a lawyer for the children, and must accept the decision of the judge. Litigated custody disputes are often long and costly, and usually create great stress for the entire family.

The more money family members have, the longer the cases can drag on, sometimes throughout a child's important growing-up years. (Lawyers' fees may range from tens of thousands of dollars to hundreds of thousands! Expert witnesses such as psychologists and psychiatrists may do evaluations [see chapter 7] that cost two to five thousand dollars or more.) Because children are involved, parents sometimes lose all objectivity and prolong the litigation. One strategy is to complicate the process further by taking the child to another state—often against the order of the court. Making the custody dispute an interstate matter can truly snarl the litigation and ensure further delays. Some parents go even further and illegally take the child out of the country. (See chapter 8 for a discussion of parental kidnapping.)

Sometimes disputes that have been settled are reactivated when one parent again becomes annoyed or frustrated with the other. The Clayburns were a perfect example of this. After a three-year custody dispute that cost Mr. Clayburn over $75,000 (he paid for his wife's lawyer as well), custody of Brian, now seven years old, was awarded to Mary Clayburn. Robert Clayburn was granted overnight visitation every Wednesday night and alternate weekends from Friday at 5 P.M. until Sunday at 5 P.M. The arrangement seemed to work for about six months. Then Mary Clayburn began to claim that Brian did not want to see his father. She said he had an upset stomach. Then she said he had too much homework. Exasperated, Mr. Clayburn began to withhold child support payments. Mrs. Clayburn took him back to court, and lawyers for both sides filed motions and countermotions. The judge finally ordered a child psychiatrist to evaluate the family and make recommendations. This delayed things further, because the psychiatrist the judge wanted was on vacation. Finally, the evaluation was done. It cost $3,200. The psychiatrist's court testimony cost another $1,500. He recommended that custody remain with Brian's mother but that she stop impeding Mr. Clayburn's visitation. She agreed, and things seemed to run smoothly for about a year.

Then the same thing started to happen again. Mary Clayburn stopped Brian's visits—sometimes at the last minute. Robert Clayburn went back to court. Six months later—after more motions and countermotions—the same judge, furious with Mary, gave custody to Robert. By this time, Brian was in trouble at school and was having behavior problems in the neighborhood: he was cursing at girls who lived on his block and threatening to hurt them if they told their parents. Mr. Clayburn began to get complaints from his neighbors. Brian began to see a psychotherapist.

CUSTODY DISPUTES SOMETIMES fuel themselves in a seemingly never-ending cycle of animosity and anxiety. Why does this happen? The most common issues in custody disputes fall into these general categories: (1) one parent believes that the other has abused the child emotionally and/or physically, (2) one parent believes that the other parent's lifestyle is not in the child's best interests, (3) one parent believes that the other has a serious psychiatric illness that interferes with parenting, (4) one parent asserts that the other has never in the past shown any interest in or responsibility for the care of the child.

Sometimes the reasons that compel parents to engage in a contest for custody are less than legitimate. For instance, a parent might not even have considered a custody challenge until a grandparent intervenes and presses for it. Sometimes, fearing that he may be denied adequate visitation rights, a father may sue for custody as a negotiating point to frighten his wife into accommodating him in the divorce settlement. All too often, parents sue for custody simply out of vindictiveness toward each other. Sometimes, emotionally vulnerable in the process of separation, they misinterpret comments the child makes and convince themselves that they should fight for custody for "the sake of the child."

Since a litigated custody battle involves legal strategies designed to win for a client, there is often a push to move quickly into battle positions, because before judges can issue the final custody decree, they usually have to make some immediate determination about temporary custody. The judge will probably incline toward the parent with whom the child is currently living. Often, this turns out to be the mother. Lawyers know that because these cases tend to last months or years, a temporary arrangement may in fact turn into a permanent one, because later on the judge might be reluctant to make a change that would disrupt the child's home life. Knowing this, lawyers usually advise their clients to stay in the marital home. The idea is that by remaining with the child, the parent will be protected against any accusation of abandonment.

If one parent does move out, however, a temporary visitation schedule is usually arranged. Sometimes the court orders a particular schedule, and sometimes parents can work one out on their own. If every decision at this time has to be a litigated one—that is, one involving the court—then it does not bode well for an easy outcome to the custody dispute. The more parents involve the court, the more they come to accept the adversarial system as the standard for resolving conflicts.

The judges have tremendous power in this system. They make the important decisions; there is no jury in custody cases. Some judges are quite adept at family law, child development, marital relationships, and psychology. They know about children and the stresses and strains of divorce and custody disputes, and have great empathy for such families. Other judges, however, are deficient in knowledge of this area of law and of human behavior in general. They may make uninformed judgments and hold opinions based upon bias rather than knowledge. The judges are thus the great undetermined factor in these disputes. Some lawyers know their judges very well and can offer theories about what you can expect. For example: "We're lucky Judge Carter is hearing this case. She's divorced, her husband doesn't pay child support, and she likes mothers," or, "We have to be very careful with Judge Meltzer. He's tough on working mothers. He thinks women belong in the home when they have young children. He still believes in the 'tender years.' " Some large law firms now use computers to search a judge's decisions for patterns that might benefit or harm a particular side. The judges' importance cannot be overstated.

The judges decide when cases will be heard and whether or not to call in an expert witness. Judges ask such experts (usually specially trained psychologists or psychiatrists) to assess the emotional status of the family members and to offer an opinion about the best living arrangement for the child. Sometimes the decision is easy; one parent may truly be unfit. But when both parents are clearly fit to care for the child, when both seem to be decent people and love the child very much, the judge has a very difficult task.

After the custody decision, the judge sets up a reasonable visitation schedule. Often the noncustodial parent will request virtually unlimited access to the child, citing the importance of the relationship to both parent and child. The custodial parent will often try to limit visitation as much as possible, sometimes secretly hoping the other parent will just go away. The judge may work out a visitation arrangement that leaves neither party happy. The child, as usual, gets caught in the middle.

In addition, the judge must rule on a child support plan when there is one custodial parent. Often one parent will have significantly more assets than the other, and child support will become yet another issue to be litigated and relitigated for years. It is often used as a wedge by one parent to get concessions from the other. And it is common for children, as they grow older, to become more aware of such financial disputes. Self-centered parents may involve the child directly. One child, thoroughly briefed by his mother about his father's alleged stinginess, told a therapist: "My father always lies when he talks to the judge. Mom and I know he has more money. He's hiding it so the judge won't know. Mom and I don't have enough money for nice clothes and vacations. My father is keeping it all. He's just a liar."

What custody arrangements can the judge order? The answer is theoretically quite simple, although getting to it may seem interminable and unbearable: either one parent assumes the entire legal responsibility for raising and providing for the child or children (sole custody) or both parents share this commitment (joint custody). Usually each parent believes (at least at the beginning of a custody dispute) that he or she alone should take care of the children. Along with this belief goes its corollary: that the other parent is unfit. The custody dispute thus becomes a campaign to win possession of the child by magnifying the positive qualities and accomplishments of one parent and denigrating the other. It seems logical that each parent will want sole custody, since the marriage has failed and chances are that they are not on the best of terms.

On the other hand, it may still be possible for both parents to share equally in the childrearing. Joint custody allows both parents to maintain a continuing and close contact with the children after the divorce. For such an arrangement to work, these parents must be able to communicate. They must be able to work out their own living and visitation arrangements. In some joint custody situations, children live with each parent for a set period of time, moving back and forth between homes. In other arrangements, the children live with one parent (at least when they are young), but both parents have legal custody. Many organizations and some state laws assume that joint custody is in the best interests of the children, and parents may be urged to agree to it even if they have doubts about its success.

Whatever arrangements the judge chooses, the decision must be based on the concept of "the best interests of the child." The needs and wishes of the parent come second. Although parents may be distraught and anxiety-ridden about an unfavorable outcome to a custody battle, and might even run the risk of becoming depressed, the judge must give a higher priority to the needs, safety, and welfare of the child.

In one custody case in which an expert witness was testifying, the father's lawyer asked the psychiatrist if he thought that the father was depressed. "Not clinically depressed," replied Dr. Lanken, "but Mr. DeVito is certainly saddened by the possibility of losing daily contact with his child and receiving only limited visitation."

"Is it not true," asked the lawyer, "that Mr. DeVito's father once suffered a severe depression and made a suicide attempt?" Dr. Lanken answered that he was indeed given that information by Mr. DeVito.

"Isn't it true, Dr. Lanken, that depression and even suicide sometimes runs in families, and that Mr. DeVito himself might be at risk for suicide if he does not get custody of his son?"

"Objection!" roared Mrs. DeVito's lawyer. "Your Honor, we are not here to perform a psychiatric analysis of Mr. De-Vito. We are trying a custody dispute and seeking the best solution for this child's welfare. It is not appropriate to spend the court's time musing upon the psychiatric future of Mr. DeVito."

"Sustained," replied the judge. "While I certainly feel for Mr. DeVito under these trying circumstances, the issue here is what the little boy, Michael, needs—not how Mr. DeVito might feel. We can't predict what might happen. We have to decide on this child's needs and what might be in his best interests right now."

A custody dispute is a painful experience for families and a complicated one for the courts. How did it come to be that way?

□ SOME HISTORICAL □
BACKGROUND

Parents involved in custody disputes soon learn that the process has its own jargon and its own traditions. As a social institution, child custody goes back to ancient Rome. The dictionary informs us that the word "custody" is derived from the Latin *custodia,* which means "guarding." Custody is defined as the immediate charge and control exercised by a person or authority upon another. Child custody refers to the right granted a parent or other legal guardian to raise a child, to make decisions about that child's life, and to be legally responsible for the child's health and safety.

In ancient Rome, child custody was synonymous with ownership. Children were considered property, and Roman law gave the father complete control over his children, including the right to sell them or condemn them to death. The mother had no legal standing. This arrangement held for hundreds of years.

In the early 1800s, some interesting legal developments altered the father's absolute rule, even if only slightly. Gradually, the concept of the absolute rights of the father expanded to include certain responsibilities for the welfare of the children. In England, the doctrine of *parens patriae* (the country acting as parent) held that the Crown had an obligation to protect those of its citizens who had no other means of protection or of assuring their own safety and welfare. In 1817, the poet Shelley lost custody of his children as a result of his atheism and alleged "profligate conduct." Although such English legal authorities as Blackstone maintained the father's absolute right to his children, others began to examine the issue on a case-by-case basis, sometimes taking an interest in the quality of the children's lives.

In a 1773 custody dispute, Lord Mansfield, an English judge, ruled that although fathers had a natural right to their children, this particular father's right was in doubt because he was bank-

31

rupt and had not demonstrated any interest in supporting his child or contributing to his family's welfare, and had engaged in "improper conduct." Lord Mansfield decided that if the parties were unable to agree on a custody arrangement, the court would intervene to choose what seemed best for the child. This was a major departure from the doctrine of the father's absolute control, and it affirmed the government's responsibility to its citizens. Lord Mansfield's idea that parental fitness should be a determining factor in child custody cases anticipated modern trends.

In 1839, the English Parliament passed Justice Talfourd's Act, which gave the court the authority to make custody determinations for children under seven years of age. Over the next hundred years, the mother gradually came to be the preferred custodian—assuming, of course, that she was "fit." On a parallel course, children themselves were no longer thought of as miniature adults, but as unique beings who were still developing and thus in need of special attention. As children began to be studied more scientifically and the concept of stages of development evolved, there emerged the recognition that they needed adequate physical and emotional nurturing in order to become healthy adults. By 1925, the Guardianship of Infants Act declared that mothers and fathers in England had an equal legal right to the custody of their children.

During the nineteenth century in the United States, a similar conflict prevailed in custody cases—this time between the ancient absolute right of the father and the more modern belief that mothers were better parents, especially with younger children. For legal purposes, this latter concept came to be known as the "tender years" presumption. (The precise length of time of the "tender years" was never spelled out, although most agreed that it applied to the ages from birth to seven.)

The view that the mother was the preferred parent had gradually gained acceptance throughout the 1800s, although the development was not straightforward. For example, a mother might be regarded as preferred, but only if she were first perceived as "fit," and the definition of fitness rested upon value judgments and moral issues. Thus, a woman divorced on the grounds of having committed adultery might lose custody of her children; other grounds included findings that a mother abused alcohol, or engaged in a style of life "abhorrent" to the court.

Some courts held that although a mother ought to be the primary caregiver for a young child, her sole custody should be limited to the early years only. In a New York custody case in 1840, for example, a mother was awarded custody of her twenty-three-month-old daughter, but the father won custody two years later. In Virginia in 1872, a three-year-old girl was given to her mother, but a year later the court held that the "tender nursing period" had passed, and the child now needed the father for "moral training." In New York in 1905, a court awarded custody of a three-year-old boy to the mother; two years later, custody was given to the father, who was felt to be entitled to it because of his "paramount right in law."

Other judicial opinions reflected the view that each case needed to be evaluated on its own merits. The judge, acting as fact-finder, would have to implement the state's role as *parens patriae* and protect each child as necessary. Those who sought a simpler way to settle custody disputes focused on the "tender years" presumption.

In general, young children—and, until the midtwentieth century, girls of any age—were increasingly awarded to the mother. As society's concern shifted toward children, and as child psychology gained acceptance as a legitimate discipline, the role of the mother became paramount in the judicial system's perception of child development. She became the preferred custodial parent. Many judicial decisions waxed eloquent about the special love only a mother could give.[1]

□ THE ''BEST INTERESTS'' □
DOCTRINE

By the latter part of the twentieth century, however, opposition to the "tender years" presumption was growing. Social and legal experts viewed it as a sexist doctrine, possibly even a violation of the Fourteenth Amendment's guarantee of equality. In most states, the doctrine has now lost favor as the primary guiding principle, although it is sometimes still invoked when both parents seem to be equally fit. Several court decisions in New York, for example, have directly criticized the "tender years" presumption and have favored the view that custody should be given to whichever parent is better able to meet the child's needs. One court even cited the work of the anthropologist Margaret Mead, which suggested that fathers as well as mothers can provide essential nurturing for the child. And as fathers demonstrated that they were capable of providing good parenting for even very young children, courts gradually came to adopt a new standard for settling custody conflicts, the "best interests of the child."

What does this mean? Most states, in fact, do not specify criteria for determining the best interests of the child, or even how to evaluate whatever criteria are being used. A judge may find it easy to determine what is *not* in a child's best interests— being abused or neglected by a parent, for example—but in the absence of such dramatic indicators, there is no real consensus. Perhaps one of the more eloquent definitions of the "best interests" presumption was offered by Judge C. J. Wilentz of the New Jersey Supreme Court. In 1988, his court heard the famous Baby M case on appeal. One argument advanced in favor of the Sterns, the couple challenging the custodial rights of the "birth mother," Mary Beth Whitehead, was that they were better educated and likely to provide a more intellectually stimulating home for the child than her natural mother. Responding to this argument, Judge Wilentz wrote in his decision:

"Best interests" does not contain within it any ideal-
ized life-style; the question boils down to a judgment, consisting of many factors, about the likely
future happiness of a human being. . . . Stability,
love, family happiness, tolerance, and, ultimately,
support of independence—all rank much higher in
predicting future happiness than the likelihood of a
college education. . . .[2]

The "best interests" presumption is child-centered rather than
parent-centered. It concerns itself with the effect upon the child
of being with one or the other parent, rather than the effect
upon a parent of "winning" or "losing." Since the doctrine is
based on the needs of the specific child, it becomes the court's
responsibility to discover what those needs are. The judge will
therefore consider the physical, material, and emotional needs
of the child, and may enlist a child behavior expert in order to
help assess these needs. The judge will examine the child's relationship with the parents as well as the child's own desires
regarding custody. No longer do most judges always assume
that the mother is the preferred parent—or even that the biological parent should always receive custody.

In one case, a New York City Family Court judge ruled that
an unmarried mother could not move to Florida to open a
business because it would deny her children easy access to their
father. The court found it in the best interests of the children
that they see their father regularly. On the other hand, a New
York State Appellate Division Court allowed a mother's request to move to California with her child and her new husband
despite the opposition of the child's biological father. This
court determined that the child had an excellent relationship
with the stepfather and the promise of a better life in California,
and that access to his biological father therefore would have to
be limited. In Arkansas, a 1987 state law allowed an unmarried
father to petition for custody, with the determining factor again
being the child's best interests.

The "best interests" doctrine has also been invoked to grant grandparents the right to petition the court for custody and visitation. In the last two decades, with the increasing divorce rate, grandparents have become more vocal and political in maintaining relationships with their grandchildren and most states now allow grandparents the right to sue for custody or visitation. (Prior to this, grandparents had virtually no rights within the court system to gain access to their grandchildren.) In New Mexico, for example, grandparents can now petition for visitation if one or both of a child's parents are deceased, or if a grandchild had previously lived with the grandparents for six months prior to removal by a parent. Grandparents in New Mexico also have standing to win a custody case—even over the child's parent—if they can prove to the judge that their guardianship is in that child's best interests.

The issue of parental morals and belief systems has come under this presumption as well. In the past, a mother or father might be denied custody because she or he was found to be an atheist, a drunkard, an adulterer, or otherwise morally want-ing. Today, for the most part, the issue before the courts is not simply parental behavior or belief, but how these factors might affect the child's best interests. Thus, the Utah Supreme Court ruled in 1987 that a parent's practice of polygamy was not in and of itself grounds for awarding custody to the other parent. And in 1986, a New Jersey Superior Court held that a custodial mother could not restrict her children's visitation with their father simply because he was cohabiting with a female friend. The court noted that in this case there was no evidence that the children were being harmed by these visits. Further, the father was judged to have a long-standing and stable relationship with his companion. Judges have also applied the "best interests" presumption to such special issues as parental homosexuality and nonbiological parents (see chapter 8).

A judge's view of the best interests of the child may be a reasonable one, or it may be idiosyncratic and largely based upon particular values and biases. Sometimes courts appropri-ately apply scientific data from the social sciences and sometimes they misinterpret this kind of research. Occasionally, the "best interests" doctrine is applied to truly bizarre situations, like the rather macabre case reported by the Associated Press in the summer of 1988. Two midwestern teenagers, a seventeen-year-old girl and her fourteen-year-old brother, were taken from their mother after authorities (acting as *parens patriae*) discovered that the family had been "looking after" the corpse of their father, who had been dead for nine years. Their mother believed that if the corpse were well tended, the family would be able to communicate with the deceased and eventually bring him back to life. Six months later, the children were returned to the mother's custody. The judge apparently decided that in spite of these grotesque family practices, the children's best interests would be served by allowing them to return to their mother.

□ THE LEAST DETRIMENTAL □ ALTERNATIVE

The "best interests" doctrine is the latest judicial standard used to decide the child placement conflicts. But, although it has been hailed as a child-centered and noble orientation for judges to follow, it is not without its critics. In 1973, Sonja Goldstein, Anna Freud, and Albert J. Solnit published *Beyond the Best Interests of the Child,* a book destined to have a profound impact on the debate over child placement.[3] Drawing from their combined backgrounds in law, psychoanalysis, and psychiatry, the authors challenged the "best interests" presumption as not going far enough to protect children.

The authors maintain that the term "best interests" suggests that a positive, therapeutic solution can be found for these complicated cases and that children will benefit from it. They aver, however, that these children are already victims at great risk, and that quick action is necessary to prevent further psychological damage. They note that the "best interests" presumption, in spite of its name, often subordinates the child's interests to those of adults, for decisions in child placement were still being made to meet the needs of parents and other litigating adults.

Beyond the Best Interests of the Child offered a new principle to guide decisionmakers: the "least detrimental alternative." This principle recognizes that there may be several options in a specific situation, but that they all may cause some harm and put the child at various degrees of risk. The authors maintain that the use of "least detrimental" instead of "best interests" could allow legislatures, courts, and childcare agencies to acknowledge "inherent detriments" in child placement decisions and could reduce the mistaken belief that "best"—as in "best interests"—means something "good" for the child. They strongly believe that swift consideration of available alternatives and rapid placement of the child is the best way to a proper disposition of these difficult cases.

Goldstein, Freud, and Solnit also propose that children should live permanently with the adult judged to be their "psychological parent." This adult is defined as the "one who, on a continuing, day-to-day basis, through interaction, companionship, interplay, and mutuality, fulfills the child's psychological needs for a parent, as well as the child's physical needs. The psychological parent may be a biological, adoptive, foster, or common-law parent, or any other person . . ." It is rare, the authors note, for young children to be able to avoid confusion and extreme anxiety during a custody battle, and extremely unlikely that they can maintain a secure alliance with both parents, who are themselves struggling with each other. Thus, they recommend that in general, custody disputes be decided in favor of the one psychological parent. Even more strongly, the authors maintain that custody decisions should be final and not open to relitigation.

Not surprisingly, this book generated heated debate. Seventeen years after publication, its major premises are still contested and argued. Some critics have protested that the concept of the one psychological parent is more theoretical than factual, and is not based upon any real behavioral or social attachments. Those who dispute the authors' contentions have also taken issue with their assertion that the custodial parent alone should make all decisions relating to visitation with the noncustodial parent, and that the courts should remove themselves from this aspect of the conflict. Many who work in the field of child placement have observed that litigating parents cannot be trusted—or even expected—to reach equitable visitation agreements on their own. Parents often play out their ongoing conflicts around the issue of visitation, using it as a wedge to force resolution of outstanding legal disputes. And parents who have custody often admit to denying their ex-spouses easy access to their children. Finally, critics of the Goldstein, Freud, and Solnit approach argue that the authors have failed to consider the importance to a child of a continuing relationship with *both* parents. This point of view finds some support in the research findings of Dr. Judith Wallerstein on the long-range effects of divorce on children discussed earlier.

Beyond the Best Interests of the Child has probably attracted more critics than proponents. Nevertheless, its authors, long-time advocates for children, have consistently asserted what many in the field have been too timid to admit: divorce and custody disputes can be highly damaging experiences for a child and require speedy action to prevent further harm; courts are hardly satisfactory agents for resolving these disputes; and tensions and conflicts inevitably surround visitation agreements in which parents remain antagonistic toward each other. In fact, few of the book's critics would argue with its assertion that a judicial order which forces visitation, or pressures parents to agree to joint custody, may represent pure fantasy by the court that everything will thenceforth be fine. However, the notion of the "least detrimental alternative," in spite of some powerful arguments put forth by its advocates, has not taken hold.

□ ALTERNATIVES TO THE □ CUSTODY BATTLE

For all its imperfection, we still rely primarily on the adversary process to resolve child custody disputes. In recent years, however, three options developed from experience with the "best interests" presumption have been introduced to mitigate the damage these conflicts often cause. The first is mediation, which is the subject of the next chapter. The other two are the "guardian *ad litem*" and joint custody.

The guardian *ad litem* ("guardian for the suit") is a person appointed by the court—sometimes at the request of a litigant —to serve as the child's advocate in custody disputes. Often a lawyer, and known to the judge as someone who has a particular interest in children, the guardian often conducts a separate investigation to come to an independent recommendation about the best disposition of the case for a particular child. In addition to reviewing reports of expert witnesses and talking with parents, teachers, and other involved parties, the guardian *ad litem* can cross-examine witnesses during the court hearing. Sometimes the guardian acts as mediator in an attempt to help the litigants reach an out-of-court settlement that will be in the child's best interests. Some jurisdictions allow the guardian to act as the child's lawyer, perhaps arguing in favor of a particular parent as sole custodian because that is what the child wants. (Certain states provide for the appointment of lawyer specifically to represent the child.)

Proponents of the guardian *at litem* approach have argued that this individual is the one person who is free of legal and emotional baggage and who can thus best safeguard the rights of the child. They emphasize the fact that in custody disputes, the primary focus of parents and their lawyers is on the adults, and that even the judge may not be sensitive enough to look out for the needs of the child.

Critics of the concept argue that it introduces yet another unknown into the already complex equation of the custody dispute and may therefore complicate the situation even further. As with some judges, lawyers, and other experts, the guardian *ad litem* may not be particularly qualified for this kind of work. The judge may happen to like a particular person and may erroneously believe that the individual's credentials are appropriate. Or the guardian may be too easily influenced by the lawyer for one side and may not be able to be an objective advocate for the child.

If a guardian *ad litem* is being considered by the judge, or if you are thinking about suggesting that someone assume that role, look into their credentials very carefully and also check your state's judicial policy for information about the function such a person will have in your case. Make sure the person is familiar with this kind of case, is knowledgeable about and comfortable with children, and seems likely to protect your child's interests. Is she a lawyer? Has she demonstrated expertise in family law cases? Is she familiar with the custody laws in your state? Does she have a bias about any particular form of custody? If she is not a lawyer, what specific qualifications have led to this appointment? For example, is she a therapist, such as a psychiatric social worker, trained to work with children and families? Does she know how to conduct interviews with young children? In what other types of cases has this person participated? Most important, is the guardian a warm, decent, and caring person you can trust to protect your child?

THE OTHER FAIRLY recent concept introduced into the field of child placement is joint custody, also called "shared custody" or "co-parenting." This phrase has become a buzzword for a whole new way of dealing with custody disputes. Joint custody refers to an arrangement in which the court recognizes *both* parents as having legal custody of the child, with equal rights and responsibilities.[4] Both share in the major decisions regarding the child's growth and development. Both have an equal voice in planning the child's schooling, medical care, religious education, and important events in the child's life.

Joint custody does not, however, automatically imply anything about the actual living arrangements for the child. That is a separate matter which both parents agree to work out and honor. The child could live with each parent alternately for a specified number of days or weeks; the child could live with each parent continually for a larger block of time, with the parents moving in and out of the home while the child remains in one place; or the child could live with one parent while the other has frequent and easy access.

Mental health professionals, legal authorities, politicians, and childcare experts have joined in the debate over this alternative. Taking into account research data suggesting that both parents can provide proper nurturing for the child, the practice of joint custody has been hailed by many as a way of eliminating the idea of "winners" and "losers," of significantly reducing the harm done by divorce, and of guaranteeing the child a continuing relationship with both parents.

The joint custody concept has also been adopted by state legislatures around the country. Most make some provisions for this kind of alternative in family law statutes. In 1987, Wisconsin enacted a law that provides for court-imposed joint legal custody even without the agreement of both parents. However, joint custody—like all legal arrangements—is no panacea; its success depends less upon the letter of the law than upon the good will and good faith of the litigating parties.

□ WHAT YOU NEED TO KNOW □
ABOUT JOINT CUSTODY

If you are considering this solution to your custody problem, your lawyer can advise you about your own state's approach to joint custody. What follows will help you to be well informed about this alternative so that you will be able to make intelligent and sensitive choices for yourself and your child.

Most mental health professionals today acknowledge that every custody dispute must be approached on a case-by-case basis. The needs of the particular child—as well as the individual characteristics of the parents—must be evaluated carefully before a plan can be proposed. That is why judges so often rely on childcare experts to help assess families. Beyond this, it appears that joint custody may succeed if a number of factors are present. First, both parents must be in favor of it. This may sound obvious, yet there are judges (and now some state legislatures as well) ready to impose joint custody over the objections of one or both parents. Such an arrangement is fraught with danger and can lead to endless problems for all members of the family.

Several further conditions must be met. One of the most important is that the parents must be able to maintain a relatively friendly relationship with each other. Certainly they do not have to be buddies, but they ought to be able to speak with each other regularly without rancor, otherwise the child will pick up on whatever tension is present between the adults and be burdened by it.

Not only should both parents have put aside much of their anger and disappointment in each other, they should also have been able to get on with their lives enough to find fulfillment elsewhere. This does not mean that they have to be remarried or even deeply involved with someone else. It does mean that they should have some gratification in their lives beyond that of simply being a parent and should be able to see themselves as more than just someone's ex-spouse.

Successful joint custody arrangements also require that both parents agree to remain within a reasonable distance of each other. They will need to be regularly involved in their child's life and able to make informed, on-the-spot decisions. This is also important for the child, who may have to travel regularly between parental households. The traveling time should be short and should not create any undue pressure for the child. Finally, joint custody is a legitimate alternative when each parent is able to tolerate the other's style of parenting. For example, if a child is allowed to watch two hours a day of television cartoons at his father's house but only a half-hour at his mother's, the difference should not become an issue between the parents. Both must be reasonable enough to realize that they will often deal with their child in different ways.

What are the drawbacks? For one thing, if one or both parents agree to it only half-heartedly, joint custody can create a host of problems for the child. Anything less than a full commitment to the arrangement creates the potential for constant tension between the parents, certain to be felt by the child as well. From the child's point of view, joint custody involving moving between parental homes has the potential for being disruptive and anxiety-provoking. Depending upon temperament and past experiences, some younger children may have difficulty moving back and forth. For older children, traveling between homes often means that they are constantly hauling clothes and schoolbooks from one house to another. The likelihood of at least some differences in the rules and routines of the two homes could cause confusion and uncertainty. And children are often made anxious by unspoken pressure from their parents not to upset the delicate balance achieved by the arrangement. Children who have experienced their parents' fighting will often go to great lengths to prevent more of it and may expend a great deal of energy in "peacemaking."

EVIDENCE IS ACCUMULATING in support of what mental health professionals have been observing for quite some time: there is no proof that children living under joint custody do any better than children in sole custody arrangements. In March 1988, preliminary results from a new study of post-divorce children were reported at the annual meeting of the American Orthopsychiatric Association. Research data gathered by the Center for the Family in Transition at Corte Madera, California, suggested that children whose parents had divorced in a relatively amicable fashion were doing relatively well psychologically regardless of the custody arrangement. Children were not doing well if they were in a joint custody arrangement ordered by the courts over parental objections, or if their parents were constantly in conflict.

In other words, the psychological status of these children of divorce was related not to their custody situation, but to the quality of their relationship with their parents and their parents' relationship with each other. The lesson seems to be that no one particular custody arrangement by itself offers any clear advantage to the child. The decisive factor is the quality of the family relationships following the divorce. This is probably the central point to bear in mind as you consider engaging in custody proceedings for your child. Joint custody may work well for some families when other important circumstances are favorable, and these circumstances are what you must consider when you are trying to decide whether or not it will work for you.

MEDIATION

3

THE ADVERSARIAL APPROACH as a means of set-
tling child custody disputes leaves much to be desired; in fact,
the legal process itself may magnify the already destructive
impact of the divorce upon the family. This chapter explores
mediation as an alternative that may prevent prolonged and
damaging conflict.

Mediation for divorcing couples emerged as an option in the
1970s, when divorce and custody laws were revised throughout

the United States.[1] Legislators, lawyers, and therapists concluded that with the rising divorce rate, new ways would have to be found to reduce the animosity and the often bitter litigation between divorcing partners. Judicial systems in California, Minnesota, and Wisconsin began experimenting with conciliation courts, where parents were encouraged to work out divorce and custody conflicts. In Alaska, Connecticut, Colorado, Iowa, Florida, Massachusetts, Michigan, New Jersey, and Pennsylvania, statewide mediation services are now available to parents who wish to make use of them. And Delaware, California, and Maine have introduced mandatory mediation in all cases of contested custody. There are also many local divorce mediation programs around the country, dedicated to helping divorcing couples settle their disputes out of court.

The American Association for Mediated Divorce (AAMD) was founded in 1980 by a psychologist, Dr. Marilyn Ruman, and her attorney husband, I. Richard Ruman, to facilitate and encourage this approach. The organization advocates a co-mediation team process in which an impartial lawyer and an impartial mental health clinician meet with the divorcing couple to help them resolve their conflicts about the dissolution of the marriage and the custody of the children. The idea behind this approach is that the lawyer can advise the couple of their legal alternatives, while the therapist helps them deal with the emotional aspects of the divorce. An attempt is made to reduce anxiety, animosity, frustration, and disappointment so that the couple can deal effectively with the legalities and come to some closure.

In actual practice, mediation is conducted in a variety of different ways. Although the AAMD suggests co-mediators, in some cases—depending on individual choice, the mediator's style of practice, and public policy—there is only one person. That person may be a lawyer with some (or no) psychological training, a psychotherapist with some (or no) legal background, a psychiatrist, a psychiatric social worker, or even a minister, priest, or rabbi, if they have had some training in mediation. Some mediations may last weeks or months; others may be completed in four or five sessions. Many mediators actually include children in some of the sessions or encourage parents to discuss plans with their children so that the whole family is informed about what is going on.

In the AAMD process, couples are first screened to determine their suitability as candidates for mediation, and their motivation and ability to negotiate with each other are assessed. If a couple seem appropriate and are willing to begin the process, they sign a premediation agreement (in which they agree to undertake mediation) and begin work. If the subsequent sessions are successful, a final agreement is drafted, reviewed by each person's lawyer, and then submitted to the court.

The AAMD agreement is divided into three parts, which together essentially set up a joint custody arrangement. The central assumption of the agreement is that both parents will successfully set aside their anger and work together for their children's best interests. Part 1 reaffirms the need for both parents to be actively involved with their children after the divorce and stresses the necessity for mutual cooperation in this endeavor. In Part 2, both parents agree to share the duties of parenting and to cooperate when decisions have to be made. In this section, the couple make plans for living arrangements and visitation schedules. Part 3 includes a foundation on which to base agreement about financial issues and provides for future mediation should problems arise.

How successful is the mediation alternative?[2] As measured by the number of custody cases that end up back in court, mediation works quite well. According to a study conducted in Toronto in the early 1980s, only 10 percent of mediated couples returned to the courtroom after two years with problems related to custody or visitation, while 26 percent of the nonmediated couples did so.[3] And couples who went through mediation were three times as likely to report better postdivorce relationships with their ex-spouses than the nonmediated couples. In a study sponsored by the Colorado Bar Association, 60 percent of couples in mediation were able to resolve their conflicts, and even those who could not do so reported better communication.⁴ Seventy percent of mediating couples agreed to joint custody. (But remember that children living in joint custody arrangements do not necessarily do better than children in other custody arrangements.) One large study, the Denver Mediation Project, conducted in the early 1980s, found mediation particularly successful in keeping divorcing families out of court. Parents who participated generally perceived mediation to be a satisfying experience, and in the short-term at least, it led to a lower rate of relitigation than proceedings handled only by the court.

Maine is one of the three states (along with Delaware and California) that have established court-mandated mediation for divorce and custody disputes. The Maine program—in effect since 1984—is relatively refreshing in its use of language: the term "custody" has been replaced by "parental rights and responsibilities," and mediators refer to the concept of joint custody as "shared parenting"—meaning joint decisionmaking and shared involvement in the growth and development of the child.

After a divorce motion is filed, the parties' lawyers, through the district or the superior court, arrange a mediation date. Maine usually assigns one mediator to the process; no background or training has been specified by the state law, and mediators may come from quite varied disciplines. The parties pay a one-time mediation fee (it was $60 in 1988) that entitles them to as many sessions as it takes to reach a settlement. (The balance of the mediator's fee is paid from state revenues.)

Surprisingly, the average number of mediation sessions is only 1.5. Because lawyers play an active role from the start, many of the disputed issues have already been discussed prior to the actual mediation. The lawyers actually sit in on the mediation sessions, so new issues can be discussed on the spot. If mediation succeeds, one of the lawyers will translate the settlement into legal language that will eventually become the court order.

What success has Maine had with this mediation program? It works quite well in terms of reducing the number of custody trials: about 25 percent of the mediated cases go on to litigation, but not all of the other 75 percent are resolved. Some of this group may go on to further mediation; others may put the process on hold for a while.

In central Kentucky, courts refer divorcing families to a special Family Mediation and Evaluation Clinic at the University of Kentucky Medical Center. About seventy families a year have been evaluated, with the average mediation process taking eight to ten sessions. The goals of this mediation are to reduce parental conflict, to develop a program assuring children of continued regular contact with both parents, to encourage the ongoing psychological relationships between the children and other significant family members, and to maintain some regular routine for the children. Families are first seen in an attempt at reconciliation. If that fails, mediation begins. If that fails as well, the family is evaluated to provide the court with specific recommendations that could help the parties involved. A one-year study of this mediation service found that 47 percent of cases were successfully settled by the parties involved. Couples who were unsuccessful in reaching a mediated solution were nevertheless supportive of the process: in the remaining 53 percent of cases, a specific plan for custody and visitation was presented to the court by the mediators.

Another study conducted fairly recently at the University of Virginia compared two groups of families: twenty families that went for mediation and twenty families that opted for litigation.[5] Mediation sessions were held at a courthouse and were limited to six two-hour sessions. The average mediation in this study was completed after 2.4 sessions. The sessions were run by male and female co-mediators whose education consisted of at least a master's degree in a mental health discipline as well as additional training in mediation skills. Both groups of families were interviewed after their disputes had been resolved.

The results showed that mediation had apparently reduced by 67 percent the number of custody disputes that ended up in court. Fifteen of the twenty mediating families were able to reach verbal or written agreement, while only five of the twenty litigating families reached an out-of-court settlement. In the litigated cases, mothers gained sole custody in eighteen of the twenty families. Although the mediation led to more joint custody settlements, it too favored custody by the mother.

What happened to these groups after the conflict was resolved? Seven members of the litigation group and eight families in the mediation group returned to court within six months. However, a greater number of total court contacts came from the litigation group. In addition, more fathers who had litigated were overdue in child support payments than fathers in the mediation group. In 1988, responding to growing pressure for such a position, Maryland also adopted court-ordered mediation for some custody and visitation disputes. Several counties in Maryland already had experimental mediation programs in place using outside mediators or county employees, and the Maryland Bar Association, in a report issued in 1986, had stated that "mediation is the most appropriate mechanism for resolving custody disputes and getting parents to work out their differences."

According to the Maryland court order, if the parties are able to reach an agreement after mediation, a written report is prepared that can then form the basis of a judicial decision. If no agreement is reached, or if the mediator deems the parties inappropriate for mediation, the court will be so informed without further comment. What has been put into practice here is precisely the mechanism proposed by the Maryland legal association itself, a mechanism deemed "most appropriate . . . for resolving custody disputes." But is this always true? Is mediation always the most appropriate solution?

☐ MEDIATION: PRO AND CON ☐

After reviewing information they had obtained about mediation services in their city, Arlene and Bruce Lewin decided to mediate their divorce and custody dispute rather than proceed with litigation. They had two daughters, Abigail, nine, and Linda, seven. Both parents had their own businesses, and each had ample funds with which to care for the children. Mr. Lewin, who regarded himself as a "modern" father, believed that as a sole custodial parent he could provide all that the children would need. He disagreed with many of his wife's ideas about childrearing, and believed strongly that she was too lenient with the children. Mrs. Lewin saw her husband as an immature person whose earning potential was unpredictable and whose manner with the children (and others, for that matter) was often brusque and cold. Nevertheless, both parents recognized the need to reduce the trauma of the divorce for Abigail and Linda, and they sought the services of Dr. Andrew Greene, a local psychiatrist who specialized in mediating divorce and custody disputes.

With Dr. Greene's guidance, the Lewins drew up a contract which stated that they would agree to mediate their custody dispute in the best interests of their children and would make every effort to reach a nonlitigated solution. They worked out a schedule for the sessions. Dr. Greene included in these sessions another psychiatrist, Dr. Anne Fried, and the mediation began. Although some of the sessions were quite heated, nobody walked out. Both parents stuck it out, and they were able to reach a settlement. They decided on a joint custody arrangement in which the children would spend two weeks at a time with each parent. Since their homes were just a few blocks from each other, they did not believe that the transitions would present too much of a problem. They agreed to share in all the important decisionmaking about the girls, such as schooling, vacations, doctors and dentists, and so on. They agreed that they would learn to live with each other's different styles of parenting. They also agreed to the regular monitoring of this accord by the mediators, and to intermittent checking in with them.

The Lewin case turned out to be a success. Although the children experienced some anxiety through the years as they moved back and forth between their parents' homes, and occasionally complained about having to pack and unpack clothes and books so often, both girls adapted to the living arrangement quite well. Bruce and Arlene became involved in other relationships and each remarried within two years. They were happy and fulfilled in their own lives, personally and professionally. They communicated readily with each other about the children and even met for lunch or dinner to discuss family issues. They had occasional disagreements about handling certain problems with the children but in general they stuck to their original mediation plan.

Mediation does offer some clear benefits. With parents actively involved in the negotiations, the anxiety that one or both will lose the children can be substantially reduced. Mediation can help parents understand the emotional impact of divorce upon their children and can make them more sensitive to their children's special emotional needs. And as a result of having helped to create it, each spouse will be more likely to adhere to the settlement.

The mediation process also offers the possibility of being fairer than a judge. In the presence of impartial mediators, both parents can feel that they are being heard equally, and that their positions are respected. Because parents and mediators develop a relationship during the multiple sessions, the process takes on a personal, participatory quality that most courtrooms cannot offer. Sorting through the issues in this way may also help parents feel more confident as they come to depend less upon their lawyers and more upon themselves. This new sense of independence can carry over into their day-to-day handling of any issues that may arise after the formal mediation is completed.

Does this mean that mediation is the answer to your particular custody problem? Not necessarily. For all of its benefits, mediation has some drawbacks—even compared to litigation.

Sarah and Richard Alwyn were divorcing and had been unable to agree about the custody of Samantha, their seven-year-old daughter. After Samantha was born, Sarah Alwyn, an attorney, had stayed at home for a month and then resumed the practice of corporate law. Richard Alwyn, an actor, was often out of work; he stayed at home with Samantha and was essentially her primary caregiver for the first two years of her life. He and Samantha developed a very close relationship. Sarah made numerous business trips and spent many late nights at the office.

When Richard landed a part in an important and successful stage play, the couple was confronted for the first time with finding regular, adequate day care (and sometimes evening care) for Samantha. Tension built. When Richard learned that Sarah was having an affair with a colleague at her firm, he filed for divorce. Sarah immediately asked for sole custody of Samantha; Richard refused. Neither could agree on joint custody, and the Alwyns' dispute began. At first, each hired a lawyer and began litigating, but they eventually decided to try to work out their differences through mediation. Their lawyers agreed upon a private mediator—a man who was a pastoral counselor and an attorney. He seemed an ideal choice, and the Alwyns went to work.

Both Sarah and Richard were intelligent and motivated, but both loved their daughter very much; yet even after several months the mediator could not bring them closer to a settlement, and he was frustrated. In an unusual move, he asked the Alwyns to agree to an impartial evaluation by a child psychiatrist. They agreed, and indicated that they would abide by the psychiatrist's recommendations. They were tired of the whole process, they said; they did not wish to pursue the adversarial approach and they were concerned most of all about Samantha. The psychiatrist was encouraged by these comments and following the evaluation, in which she saw both parents and the child several times, she concluded that Samantha's father should have sole custody, but that her mother should be granted liberal access.

Naturally, Richard Alwyn was delighted. But Sarah was furious. She charged that the mediator was not objective at all, that he had taken Richard's side in arguments and worse, that he had sent them to a "profather" psychiatrist. Sarah attacked the mediation process as being pointless, boring, and completely one-sided. She refused to participate in any further mediation or negotiation and instructed her lawyer to go ahead and litigate the case. She could not be mollified, and the Alwyn case became an extremely long and frustrating custody dispute.

It would be unfair to conclude that this case turned out badly because of the mediation process itself. Given the stubbornness of the disputing parties, an out-of-court settlement might well have been impossible regardless of the route taken. Yet it is clear that the unsuccessful mediation only deepened the Alwyns' anger and discontent, and their case illustrates some of the potential problems with mediation.

Those problems were succinctly addressed by Carol S. Bruch, professor of family law at the University of California at Davis, in her testimony before the New York state legislature against a bill that called for mandatory mediation of child custody and child support cases. In an article expressing the views she set forth in her testimony, Professor Bruch notes that although mediation reduces some custody litigation, a protracted, difficult, and unsuccessful mediation experience can be just as devastating as litigation to parents and children alike. One disadvantage of mandatory mediation is that it may force parents to begin to negotiate when they are simply not ready; oddly enough, litigation, with its many built-in delays and postponements, may actually allow parents time to adjust and prepare psychologically for negotiations. Moreover, children are not necessarily best represented in mediation. They are frequently excluded from the mediating process, which, when mandated, tends to consist of a limited number of sessions. During litigation, on the other hand, a guardian may be appointed to represent them, and/or they may be interviewed by the judge. Finally, Professor Bruch observes, there is no research evidence to support the claim that children whose parents mediate custody settlements do better than children of litigating parents.[6]

Today, certain expectations surround the mediation alternative that are either unproved or otherwise open to challenge.

For example, the assumption that mediation will lead divorcing couples away from bitterness, disappointment, and anger and toward cooperation, understanding, and tolerance has not been documented. The expectation that mediation will somehow allow both parties to represent their own points of view effectively without the assistance of counsel is similarly unfounded. Even a highly skilled mediator, Professor Bruch has pointed out, cannot compensate for the sharp differences in sophistication and power that often exist between divorcing spouses.

In her objections to mandatory mediation, Professor Bruch has addressed a matter familiar to those who follow the disposition of custody cases: that women are often at a distinct disadvantage in mediation. (It is not correct to assume that even with co-mediators, a female mediator will be sympathetic to the divorcing woman.) Professor Bruch has reported, "Attorneys have told me that . . . they will get written reports from mediators in which literally the husband is referred to as 'Mr. So-and-So,' and the wife is referred to by her first name, which suggests that the husband and his views are accorded more respect than the wife and hers. . . . In mediation, you have to be able to voice your own concerns effectively and represent them without a lawyer. When you go to court, whether your lawyer is male or female, the lawyer is supposed to state the case as vigorously for you as it can be stated. That is an appropriate role. Even if you are a very meek and mild person, you can say that your lawyer said you have to do something a certain way. You're not the person who has to speak out or be assertive. That is the role of the lawyer. In mediation, there is a lot of listening to people and letting them be heard. I am concerned that the men may be heard a lot and the women are not being heard, and that they're being talked over and not listened to."[7]

The University of Virginia study mentioned earlier tends to confirm Professor Bruch's concerns. Fathers in that study were found to be more satisfied if they had mediated their settlement than if they had litigated it. In contrast, mothers in litigation reported feeling that they had won more and lost less than did mothers in mediation. The mothers in mediation also reported more psychological distress than did the litigating mothers.

With all of this to consider, how can you determine if mediation is best for you? First, mediation might be successful in a situation where joint custody also has a chance. In other words, both parents must be able to be more than civil to each other while in the same room. You must be ready to negotiate. You must be strong enough psychologically to think clearly about the ramifications of your actions and decisions. You must be willing to set aside the frustration and disappointments of your failed marriage and shattered home life, and deal with the person you may feel is responsible for all this trouble. You must be able to tolerate each other's differences in style as well as in principles. You must also be able to put aside your own interests from time to time in order to provide the best for your children. And you must be willing to take a chance on an alternative that has not been proven to be better than litigation and that may or may not work well for you.

But . . . you may not have a choice. If your case is filed in California, Delaware, or Maine, you will be subject to mandatory mediation. Elsewhere, you may have the option of trying court-sponsored mediation or to engage in it privately. At this point, as a consumer of a very important service, you need to ask some important questions. What mediators are available and who are they? Do they work alone or with a co-mediator? What are their qualifications? Is the mediator a mental health professional? A lawyer? A member of the clergy? Has the mediator received special training in this area? Most important, do you think you can feel reasonably comfortable working with this particular mediator? Do you like her approach? Does she have any visible biases, such as favoring joint custody, or being opposed to father-only custody? Does she seem empathic and sensitive to your needs? Is she child-centered enough to remind you and the other party that there are children involved? When all is said and done, you ought to like and trust this person. If you don't, for whatever reason (whether you think you're justified or whether it's just a feeling), don't go on with it. You don't have to explain or defend yourself. You have every right to demand to feel secure and comfortable with the person acting as your mediator.

As a general rule, it's best to look for someone with some specific training in both psychotherapy *and* mediation. Even a good psychotherapist is not necessarily a good mediator. Your lawyer can help you check credentials, or you can perhaps get information from your local library and the AAMD. And do look for someone with more than just on-the-job experience. A member of the clergy may be used to giving advice, but may have no specific skills in counseling and mediation. Avoid such a person, even if you have been comforted by a minister or a rabbi in the past.

Inquire about your mediator's previous experience. What percentage of her cases have remained truly settled, and what proportion have gone on to litigation anyway, and to relitigation after that? And you should be wary of mediators who seem to operate according to some predictable pattern. For example, if mediation with a particular person always results in joint or maternal custody, or if any father desiring sole custody seems to get it, then the chances are that this mediator works from a particular bias, rather than from a position of helping parties figure out what's best for *them*. If a mediator works according to the needs of the individual parties, then there will be some variation in the outcome of the cases.

Ask how the mediation is conducted. What are the fees? Is the number of sessions determined at the outset or is the approach open-ended? Can your lawyer sit in? What are the goals for you and the other party in the mediation? Are they clear to you? Does everyone have the same objectives? Ask as many questions as you want, for you are the one who will have to feel comfortable with the ground rules. If you don't, and your geographic residence gives you a choice, don't consent to mediation.

Find out what happens when your mediation is completed. Is a written report prepared? Does it go to the judge? There should be written documentation summarizing your agreement, if any, and both parties should sign it. Make sure that you know exactly what to expect every step of the way. If you live in a state that has mandatory mediation, make sure you know that state's procedures. It will be even more important in such a case to check the credentials of the mediator(s). (In the proposed New York state legislation, the requirements for becoming a mediator were not specified. In Maine, the mandatory mediation bill was passed before there were enough mediators to undertake the work at hand; in some cases, college professors in the liberal arts were enlisted to do the job.)

Keep in mind that you must feel as if you have some control of the process. You cannot be sure of what the outcome will be, but the sense that you are fairly represented should help to relieve your anxiety as you proceed with your custody dispute.

To summarize, many disputing parties report greater satisfaction with mediation than with the adversarial system. Critics of litigation point to its tendency to pour more kerosene on an already raging fire. Lawyers—many of whom by their own admission simply love to argue—can actually compound the hurt and anger by prolonging the litigation and raising the ante. The delays which are so much a part of this system can hurt the child severely. A young child, for example, does not have a clear concept of time and may not perceive that there will be an end to the dispute. Most dangerously, with parents fighting each other so intensely, the interests of the child may not be heard at all. In the dramatic charges and countercharges typical of court proceedings, parents who at one point might have been willing to sit down and talk rationally may come to feel only intense hatred. This rage then can spill over into the relationship with the child. In addition, just as the level of competence of lawyers and mediators varies, so does that of judges. A particular judge may or may not want this sort of work, may or may not even have a notion of the most elementary aspects of child development and psychological trauma, may or may not know how to talk to a young child, and may or may not have a strong grasp of custody law. Should parents take a chance that the judge before whom they appear will be sympathetic, sensitive, and unbiased?

Perhaps you prefer not to take such a chance. In that case, an honest discussion with the other side could lead to the two of you sitting down to work out a settlement. But again, there is no hard evidence that mediation is the preferred solution to your dispute, that your position will be heard any more objectively or accurately than it might be in court, or that children whose parents mediate a custody dispute do any better in the long run than children whose parents choose litigation. We still have much to learn. The important thing, as we will see in the next chapter, is that you think *before* you act.

THINK BEFORE
YOU 4 ACT

P ARENTS GO ABOUT the processes of separation, divorce, and custody dispute in different ways. Sometimes the couple and the child or children continue to live under one roof. Sometimes one parent or a parent with the child will leave abruptly, which usually comes as a complete shock to the "abandoned" parent. No matter what happens, the child will always be affected.

Bill and Sandy Riale had been having marital difficulties for about five months. Sandy's constant complaint was that Bill was not earning enough money to support the family, which included their three-year-old daughter, Tara. Bill maintained that he brought home enough money, but that Sandy had expensive tastes. He argued that she was always trying to impress her friends and spent money frivolously on shopping sprees. Sandy denied this and accused Bill of being an alcoholic. Later she told her lawyer that Bill had come home drunk several times and once had pushed her against the kitchen door, hurting her and frightening Tara.

One Sunday afternoon, Bill went out bowling with some friends; Sandy told him she would have dinner ready when he returned. Bill came home to an empty house. His wife's car was gone, and he found a note on the kitchen table, which said that on the advice of her lawyer and with the concurrence of several of her friends, she had chosen this way to leave Bill for good. She had taken Tara with her, and in about a week she would tell Bill where they were living. In the meantime, she added, Bill would be wasting his time if he tried to find them. She promised to call and to allow him to visit Tara.

Unfortunately, Sandy did not handle the move very well with her child, as she later volunteered during a therapy session. After her husband had left the house for his bowling date, she said to her daughter, "Come on, Tara, we're going for a ride." When the child asked where they were going, Sandy said, "To a nice place for some ice cream and fun." When they arrived at the furnished apartment Sandy had secretly rented, she told Tara they were going to stay there for a while. "Why?" asked the child. "We have a nice house already. When is Daddy coming over?" Sandy told Tara that her father had gone away on a business trip for a few days. Tara soon stopped asking questions, and Sandy was relieved. She thought her daughter was doing well and had accepted her explanations. As it turned out, Tara was quite anxious about what happened. But because she could see that her questions were upsetting her mother, she had simply stopped asking them.

Bill searched for Sandy and Tara fruitlessly. He had also

retained his own lawyer. As she had promised, Sandy contacted Bill a week later and arranged for him to visit Tara. The details of the visitation were worked out by the two lawyers. Bill agreed that he would visit Tara on weekends and that she would remain with her mother during the week. Fortunately for Tara, her parents were able to come to a quick agreement, even though they were in the throes of a sudden separation and divorce proceedings.

If you are at the point of leaving your spouse, you have to decide how best to carry out the actual separation. Sometimes lawyers will recommend sudden, unexpected departures, particularly if a woman fears physical harm to herself and/or her child. If you do leave in this way, try to see such an experience through a child's eyes, and think about the consequences and how best to handle them. Some children tolerate change better than others, but in general it is better to be honest when you explain why you have decided to move. You don't need to go into great detail with a young child, but you should be as truthful as you can. You might say to a four-year-old, "We're going to be living in a new place for a while because Mommy and Daddy are not being friendly to each other. But you and I will be okay—and we'll see Daddy/Mommy real soon. . . . And to older children of perhaps seven or eight, "You know Dad/Mom and I have just not been getting along. We all need a break to calm down and not fight so much. But don't worry, you're still going to be seeing both of us." And unless you believe that you or your child are in imminent danger from the other parent, arrange for visitation as quickly as possible.

Negotiate an agreement with the other parent that takes into account your child's schedule as well as your own, and works around day care or school hours. Alternating weekend visits can give you and your child unhurried time together. Weekday visits are important too, but tend to be more rushed, given bedtimes and homework. However, the child can look forward to the regular Tuesday or Wednesday visits with the noncustodial parent. Be realistic about the time you can really spend together during the week. Consider vacations, holidays, and birthdays and work out your schedule in advance. Important holidays such as Thanksgiving, Christmas, Hanukkah or other religious holidays can be alternated yearly.

Once you enter litigation, the judge will want to set up a temporary visitation schedule anyway. Wouldn't you prefer to work out your own agreement rather than have one imposed upon you? If you are able to remain child-centered during this time, rather than becoming totally self-involved, you should be able to reach an understanding with the other parent. And by doing so, you'll have dealt successfully with one of the many arduous steps in the torturous process that is a custody dispute.

□ TAKING CHARGE □

If you're like most parents going through a crisis with your children, you have no doubt heard stories about other people's custody disputes. Perhaps you have even helped a friend through one and never dreamed that the same thing could one day happen to you. By now, well-meaning friends and anxious relatives have probably told you just what you should do next. But no matter how tempting it may be to let others steer you along, you yourself must take charge of the situation.

Jane Larkin was divorcing her husband, David, after seven years of marriage. She had met and fallen in love with someone else; the relationship was far more passionate than the one she had had with David. The Larkins had a three-year-old son, Adam. David had always been very much involved with the child, and Jane agreed that he had been a superb father. He was distraught at the breakup of his marriage.

Jane said she did not wish to harm Adam's relationship with his father. She did not want a custody battle, and believed she and David could jointly care for their son. Jane's widowed mother, however, firmly believed the divorce was David's fault. His behavior was responsible, she thought, for Jane's seeking someone else, and he would therefore also be a bad influence on Adam. She had forgotten the time she told her daughter that David was "the finest son-in-law anyone could have," and was now furious with David for ruining her daughter's life. She urged Jane to seek sole custody of Adam. "David never was such a great father," she told her daughter. "You don't need him anyway. And no matter what happens, you can always count on me."

Jane had always been close to her mother, a schoolteacher, and she respected her professional experience and her understanding of children. Still, she could not deny the fact that David was an excellent father and that he and Adam were very close. What should she do?

This is a common scenario in families as parents prepare for divorce and consider child custody. Anxiety is high, emotions are intense, and advice flows like a white-water river in the spring thaw.

Keep in mind that *no one*—including a parent, a lawyer, or a therapist—can tell you what is right. You must seek the answer within yourself. Everyone else will have a particular point of view based upon their own biases, beliefs, and experiences. And the more you seek advice from others, the more complicated the dilemma will become for you. If you do not remain true to yourself now, and do what you honestly believe is best, you are likely to be angry and disappointed later, and to regret the decisions you made on the advice of others.

In Jane Larkin's case, she decided to take charge. She told her mother that she appreciated how upsetting all this was for her and that she was glad her mother loved her grandson so much. However, she alone would make the decision about custody and would try her best to use as a guide what she thought was in Adam's best interest. She told her mother gently but firmly that the complex reasons for the divorce were her own business, and that she would work them out with Adam's father. She said that it was a sad time for the whole family—especially for Adam—and while it might seem easier to get angry and blame someone, that would not help the situation. In the midst of her own distress, Jane asked her mother to be as loving and supportive as she had always been, and to trust her, as Adam's mother, to do what was right for herself and her child.

That conversation brought Jane and her mother closer than they had ever been before. It helped to calm the older woman, who was finally able to tell her daughter how afraid she was of losing Adam altogether. A widow with only one child, she herself had few close relatives. And after they had talked, Jane too felt supported and not quite so alone as she confronted the difficulties that lay ahead.

If you are divorcing and considering a custody dispute, you probably also feel very lonely. That is certainly understandable. It is also normal to feel that things would be much simpler if someone with experience would tell you what to do. At such a time all of us are tempted to just give in and be taken care of. You need to resist this urge as much as possible. Family and friends can be major sources of help, but not because they tell you how to make your decisions. Rather, they can help ease some of the loneliness and fear that you may be experiencing now. The real work still has to be done by you; there is no way around this. But there are ways for you to help yourself as you face these difficult tasks.

The first step is to review in your own mind what has already happened. You are expecting to begin a custody dispute or are already in the middle of one. Or your husband or wife is threatening such a battle. How did you get to this point? What happened to your relationship? Why are you involved in a custody dispute? Are you angry at your spouse for what happened to your marriage? Are you afraid of something? Are you responding to pressure from your parents or to criticism from your in-laws? Did a friend or a lawyer urge you to take this action? Where does your child fit in? Separating your anger from the issue of your child's best interests is vital. Try to make some objective evaluation of your relationship with your child. Look at your spouse's relationship with the child as well. What would be the impact on the child of being parented by just one of you after the divorce? By both of you?

Next, consider your custody options. This is your most important decision. Forget about the legal questions. Forget about experts who state categorically that joint custody is the only solution in the child's best interests, or that sole custody is your only realistic choice. Forget about your charming, intelligent neighbors who have a joint custody arrangement that seems to work just fine. Forget the magazine articles and the advice from good friends and concerned relatives. Ask yourself what kind of custody arrangement *you* can live with.

You know what the studies have shown about successful joint custody arrangements. Would you and the other parent qualify? Do you already have evidence that you can sit down together and make plans for your children? Can you tolerate each other's differing styles of parenting? Can you get beyond your anger and disappointment? Do you want your children to move back and forth between homes, or do you think they would be better off in one place but with both parents actively and frequently involved with each other and with them? Only you can answer these questions honestly. And remember, there is no clear-cut evidence that children of divorce automatically do better in a joint custody arrangement.

When the Wilsons divorced, they agreed to joint custody. They wanted to spare their two boys, aged seven and nine, a custody battle, and each thought that the other would be cooperative. The Wilsons had consulted a prominent psychologist, who had advised them that their sons would suffer far less from the effects of the divorce in a joint custody arrangement. Since they lived only ten blocks from each other, it seemed a workable solution. They arranged for the boys to spend two weeks at a time with each parent. Vacations and other holidays would be divided equally. The plan seemed fine—on paper.

In reality, Etta and Frank Wilson were never able to discuss the children without becoming angry. Often, they could not keep from being openly hostile to each other as they transferred the boys from one home to the other. The two boys, over time, developed their own ways of reacting to the constant tension between their parents. Jimmy, the older one, became sullen and withdrawn. He kept to himself, did not pursue friendships, and was uncommunicative in general. The younger child, Kenneth, developed behavior problems in school: he hit other children, used foul language with his teacher, and gradually turned into a bully. Things became even worse when Etta Wilson remarried after a year. Her ex-husband was very resentful and did not try to hide his feelings from his children. He constantly criticized Etta and made insulting remarks about her new husband, whom he seemed to enjoy denouncing as a "dumb stockbroker." Clearly, no one was happy with this situation.

This kind of outcome demonstrates that even sensible plans do not always work out, no matter how good the parents' intentions. You must look into your heart and discuss the situation with the other parent—if you can—to determine whether the arrangement can work *in practice* for your family. Of course, you cannot know what the future will bring, but you must make the best possible choice based upon what you know about yourself and your former partner.

Philip and Louise Taylor had been married for eight years and had a seven-year-old girl, Amy, and a five-year-old boy, Todd. Their divorce was proceeding amicably; to the amazement of the lawyers, financial considerations were easily negotiated by both parties. Both Philip and Louise realized that the more contact each of them had with the children, the better the chance of reducing the trauma of the divorce. Although Philip moved out, he visited the children frequently during the week as well as on the weekend, and Louise welcomed his involvement. The parents, meanwhile, set about rebuilding their lives. Both worked, and now each began to socialize more often with their old friends and to make new ones. Their lives, though separate from each other, were filled with activities. Some of these included the children; others did not.

When the divorce settlement turned to the issue of custody, both Louise and Philip were certain they wanted a joint custody arrangement. They agreed that the children would feel most comfortable if they remained in their home with their mother. However, the Taylors also agreed that they should share equally in the raising of their children. They decided that when the children were older it might be okay for them to move more freely between the two homes, but for now one home was best. They agreed to discuss the need for doctors and dentists, to make joint decisions about the children's schooling, summer camp, and so on.

This arrangement actually worked out quite well over the years. Philip and Louise were able to work out most of their disagreements. Sometimes the children reported feeling under pressure to keep the peace; they would say everyone tried hard to be "polite" a lot of the time. This particular kind of stress had been reported in other children in joint custody. Nevertheless, Amy and Todd could also say without hesitation that it was nice to be able to see both of their parents often. The key for this family seemed to be that both parents had been able to get beyond the anger and disappointment of the divorce and proceed with their own lives. They had found fulfillment in other ways and had continued to enjoy their children, rather than seeing them as symbols of their own failed hopes and dreams. It is in situations like this one that children of divorce seem to have the fewest problems.

Clearly then, joint custody, while not a panacea, can offer certain families an opportunity to reduce some of the psychological trauma of separation and divorce. It didn't work for the Wilsons, but it did for the Taylors. Can it work for you?

Think now about your lawyer. As you weigh your options, be aware of the natural tendency at a time like this to want to "win" this case against your ex-spouse. That word is in quotation marks for a reason. A legal victory in a custody dispute really has nothing to do with the true outcome for you and your children. In the heat of battle, all efforts seem to be directed toward winning. This is mainly because our legal system is based upon an adversarial process. You hire a lawyer to make the best possible case on your behalf before the judge. The lawyer has one primary objective: to gain a victory for you. Many lawyers are drawn into matrimonial law and litigation because to a large measure they enjoy the battle itself, as well as the victory. And they are, in fact, bound by the ethics of the legal profession to do all in their power (and within the law) to win the case for their client.

You will want a lawyer who is competent and experienced and who knows your state's matrimonial law. Lawyers vary, though, not only in skill but also in their concern for the children caught up in a custody dispute. Usually, a lawyer will volunteer that she is extremely sensitive to the needs of the child, and that her primary concern is the welfare of the child or children involved. The wise parent takes this assurance with a grain of salt until credentials and reputation can confirm it. But your lawyer should indicate that she is responsive to your needs and desires and that you will be in charge.

As you consider what kind of custody you will seek and how you want to use your lawyer, think about your living arrangements now, before anything is settled. (This issue is particularly relevant in cities, where space is scarce and housing prices are high.) Often, the lawyers for both sides in a divorce will advise their clients not to move out of the family home. Parents are told that once they leave the house, it might be difficult to reclaim title to the property; that they could be accused of abandonment; or that leaving might complicate the custody case in other serious ways. So a mother and father, both furious with each other and embarking on the long, unhappy process of divorce and a custody battle, end up still living together. Almost invariably, the domestic situation deteriorates still further.

This was the Carters' situation. Dr. Howard Carter, a physician, and Dr. Roberta Sloane, a college professor, had been married for thirteen years and had an eight-year-old daughter, Lisa. When the Carters decided to divorce, the lawyers advised each of them not to move out of the six-room apartment they jointly owned. No one in the family liked the situation, but neither of the parents wanted to go against the lawyer's wishes.

During an evaluation, Howard Carter explained to the child psychiatrist what it was like in their household. "Roberta and I rarely speak to each other. It's just about impossible to have any kind of civil conversation with her. So I avoid it. When I come home, the usual story is that she's come home earlier and has quickly made dinner, so that I miss having supper with my daughter. She's even started to keep a separate set of dishes just for her and Lisa. My child is usually doing homework when I get in, and I don't want to interrupt her. So my time with her is limited. Roberta always wants to spend time alone with Lisa before she goes to sleep. I feel rotten about all this, and once Roberta and I had this big fight—I even pushed her—because I wanted to speak to Lisa alone. Lisa saw us and cried hysterically. I felt terrible about the whole thing. Roberta called me a bastard in front of Lisa, and at that point I just left the room. I can't stand this tension much longer. But if I move out, I could lose the whole case. And I think Lisa must be heartbroken by all this. I hate to think what the strain is doing to her. Even when Roberta and I aren't fighting, you could cut the tension in our house with a knife."

Roberta Sloane had a different view of the problem. She didn't think Lisa was suffering so much. "Lisa is a very intelligent little girl. I haven't tried to keep anything from her. I told her straight out we were getting a divorce, and I've told her that her father and I have a disagreement over where she will live. Lisa has told me that she wants to live with me, and I'm sure that the judge will go along with her wishes. I don't think there's that much tension at home. Lisa can handle it. She knows I love her and that I'll take care of her. This may go on for several more months, because my lawyer thinks there might be another delay before our court date. If that happens, Lisa and I will cope, just as we have up until now. I think Lisa's a strong girl and able to deal with this; Howard is making a big deal out of it. All he's interested in is destroying me, so naturally he would say the situation at home is horrible. I don't know, really, how he can say anything about it, since he's hardly ever home."

Lisa seemed to welcome the opportunity to speak with an impartial professional. After a first session in which she was rather reticent, she began to talk easily about her feelings. "It's weird at home. It's like we're a make-believe family. I mean, my mother and father almost never talk to each other. When they do, they almost always have a fight. Then I go to my room and try to make some other noise that blocks out their fighting. I play my music loud or I open a window so I can hear the cars outside. Sometimes I cry to myself. Why can't they stop it? I don't know who I want to live with. Sometimes I'm mad at my mother and I want to live with my dad. Most of the time, I just can't decide. I don't tell them what I'm thinking because they have their own problems. I wish they would just stop it."

After eight months, Lisa's father finally moved out. The situation in which a divorcing, battling couple still reside in the same house with the children is an untenable one for everyone. Don't assume that you and your child will be able to handle it, or that it is not such a big deal. Don't be reassured by your lawyer, who might tell you that lots of families go through this and come out fine. This type of arrangement—which, by the way, can go on for *years*—is extremely detrimental to a child. It perpetuates a condition that is both confusing and anxiety-provoking, creates enormous pressure, and forces the child to use every ounce of psychological energy to cope.

If you think that this under-one-roof residency is better than one parent moving out because it allows the child to have access to both parents, you are fooling yourself. The tension, the silences, the competition for the child's attention and affection are, in most cases, far more harmful than if one parent moved out. Ideally, neither parent should agree to this type of arrangement, no matter how persuasively a lawyer might argue for it as a necessary, and temporary, strategy. If for some reason it *has* to be this way, be especially sensitive to your children during this time. They will be sure to have strong feelings about the situation. Even if there are no overt signs of distress, you can be sure they are under great pressure.

What can you do? Tell your lawyer to use some other strategy. By moving out, you are showing that you do care about your children's welfare and you do genuinely wish to reduce family tensions. Be sure your children know that you will see them even though you are living somewhere else. Let your lawyer know how tense it's been at home and insist that your wishes be respected and understood. Even though your lawyer warns you that it will seem as if you are walking out on your children, you can document in other ways that you have had continuing contact with them even after your move. By continuing some financial support, and through frequent visits and an ongoing involvement in their school and social lives, you will demonstrate your deep connection to your children.

□ **KNOW THYSELF** □

No matter how well you seem to be coping with all these decisions, this is a time of extraordinary stress. Part of you might be feeling strong, in charge, and confident, yet a whole other side of you might simultaneously feel frightened and insecure. Be aware that separating can stir up intense feelings left over from your own childhood. Perhaps your own parents went through a divorce. Or one parent might have deserted the family or died when you were young. You might unconsciously identify with your child, who is going through a similar experience right now. Be careful that you don't confuse your own unfinished business from childhood with your child's present needs.

Tim and Jennifer Browne were divorcing. They had a nine-year-old son, Billy, and both parents had been very much involved in his growth and development. Tim, a news reporter, had always had a very busy schedule. Nevertheless, he had attended prenatal classes with Jennifer and had participated in her labor and Billy's delivery. He had arranged his schedule to spend more time at home in Billy's early years and had been a very nurturing father. When Billy was six, his parents began to have the marital problems that culminated in the divorce action. Intelligent, caring people, they planned from the start to arrange for joint custody so that Billy could have continued close contact with both of them.

Tensions between Jennifer and Tim increased, however. As negotiations began on the custody issues, Tim became extremely anxious and more and more frustrated with Jennifer. He now insisted on sole custody, certain that joint custody would never work, that Jennifer would sabotage the plan and deny him access to his son. He complained that she was "working Billy over" to lessen the child's identification with him and to increase his dependence upon her. He lost his temper with Jennifer on several occasions, cursed her in front of his son and threatened to "win" Billy away from her.

During a psychiatric evaluation by a court-appointed child psychiatrist, Tim described his own childhood. His father had left home one day when Tim was seven years old, and was never heard from again. Tim remembered how terribly unhappy he had been, and how his mother had become severely depressed and had taken to her bed for almost a year. His fourteen-year-old brother had left home soon after. It had been the most traumatic experience of Tim's life—something from which he had never completely recovered.

When he and Jennifer married, he had loved her very much and had always planned on having children. With Billy's birth, all his dreams had seemed to come true. He told the psychiatrist that the thought of losing Billy now was bringing back a flood of memories from when he had lost his father. In being a father to Billy, Tim was, in effect, undoing much of the hurt he had felt when his own father had deserted him. During this evaluation, he came to realize that to a large extent his decision to sue for sole custody had been motivated by the unresolved fears he had experienced when his father left. He could see that he had never fully worked through the emotions he had experienced as a boy, and that he was reliving those emotions through Billy and identifying with his son. The thought of doing to Billy what his father had done to him—even if this was not an exact repetition—was horrifying to him. So he had decided to gain control over the situation by refusing to work out an equitable agreement with his wife.

In this case, the psychiatric evaluation, although conducted primarily to help the judge make a decison about Billy Browne's placement, had served a therapeutic purpose for Tim Browne as well. Because he was truly a loving father and was aware of the need to protect his son from the marital conflict as much as possible, he was able to apply what he had learned about his motivations. He agreed to resume negotiations toward joint custody. He even entered psychotherapy in order to understand his feelings better and to finally put to rest the conflicts about his father that he had suppressed for so long.

One of the motivations for a parent who demands sole custody and/or insists on a custody battle might be to preserve what he or she sees as a very special relationship with a child. This parent may become jealous and be terribly threatened by the other parent's connection with the child. The other parent may be perceived as psychologically "kidnapping" the child. Such behavior may be totally unconscious, and often derives from the fact that the parent is feeling threatened in an entirely different way. The following case shows just how this might happen.

Jane Morris was divorcing her husband, Carl. They had a seven-year-old boy, Jerome. Jane and Carl had tried to have a child for more than three years and had almost given up; when Jane finally became pregnant, she was thrilled. Her own parents lived more than a thousand miles away, and she missed them. Her best friend had moved away, and Carl seemed to have so many friends of his own that she'd felt left out and isolated. She was certain that the baby would now make them a real family. During the pregnancy, she did not feel quite as lonely as she used to when her husband went off to work.

Jane and Jerome had always been very close. Now that she and Carl were divorcing, Jane was haunted by her son's having told her years before, "Mommy, I want to live alone with you, and when I grow up I want to marry you." Jane had thought his comment cute at the time, but now it seemed to take on special meaning. Yet at this point, Jerome and his father were becoming quite close. Jerome even tried to dress like his father and loved to go fishing with him; he looked forward to it every weekend. When they were out together, Jane felt utterly alone —far more so, in fact, than in the unhappy days before Jerome was born. She feared that this little boy—who looked exactly like her, by the way—was being taken out of her life.

Jane was at war with herself. On the one hand, she was glad that her son felt comfortable with his father but on the other hand, she resented the intrusion into her special relationship with the boy. At times, she even felt that Carl was deliberately trying to drive a wedge between herself and Jerome.

In fact, Jane's fears were unfounded. Her husband simply enjoyed being with his son and knew full well how deeply Jerome needed his mother. But Jane was suffering from a great deal of anxiety, and her sense of isolation was growing. Her desperate feelings, unfortunately, drove her to insist on sole custody, with extremely limited visitation for Jerome's father. Through her lawyer, Jane charged that Carl had never been close to his son and that he was using the child to further his own ends in this dispute. Carl had no choice but to refute these charges and to fight for his son in court. He too now wanted sole custody. He was afraid that without it, Jane would prevent him from seeing Jerome.

In this case, then, Jane's neediness affected her ability to make rational decisions. Asked why she was fighting so hard for sole custody, she was able to present a series of reasonable-sounding answers that made it appear she had Jerome's best interests at heart. Her intense agitation and fears for herself only came to light after two years of litigation and upon learning from her son's therapist how severely depressed her child had become. At that point, she agreed to work out an equitable joint custody arrangement with Carl.

Again, unconscious impulses can sometimes directly affect parents' behavior during divorce and custody proceedings. Some of these impulses may actually be quite sadistic—not toward the other parent, but toward the child. Does this sound surprising? In fact, some parents, in spite of what they say, harbor deep feelings of resentment toward their children. The resentment may be due to the profound changes in the adult's life after a child's birth, the apparent loss of freedom, the additional stress on the marriage, and even envy of a child for possessing anything from good looks to talents the parents feels he or she lacks.

Sometimes this resentment surfaces in obvious ways: the parent may verbally abuse, threaten, hit, or otherwise punish the child inappropriately. At other times, however, it lives deep within the parent. Sometimes it can be recognized only through intensive psychotherapy over a long period of time. But in many cases, these feelings can result in a parent making decisions that are quite detrimental to the child. It is even possible, difficult as this might be to believe, for parents to initiate or maintain a custody battle as a way of punishing their children. In many such cases, the parents simply are not aware of this dynamic and would be shocked at the suggestion.

What can you do about your unconscious? Not a whole lot, to be blunt. Even people who have undergone long-term psychoanalysis don't lose their unconscious; they simply have a better handle on why they do what they do. It's best to keep in mind that no matter how angry you are at your wife or husband and no matter what the history of your relationship has been, these feelings should not cloud your concern for your child's best interests. Your children will never see things the way either of you do. *Their* relationship with the other parent will always be quite different from yours. If you launch a campaign to try to convince them that you are the best mother or father in the world and that they do not need the other parent, you will only confuse and hurt them and add to their anxiety. Be aware of your feelings, so that whatever decision you make is influenced by the most rational, healthiest part of you. You may wish to consult a therapist yourself right now, to gain some insight and more effectively cope with the stress that lies ahead. Before you make any serious decisions about your next steps, take the time for honest self-examination.

TELLING THE
CHILDREN

When you are involved in divorce proceedings and a custody dispute, you become very self-absorbed. First there is the disorientation you experience as you face the end of your marriage and the disruption of your home life. Then comes a multitude of other feelings: profound sadness, anger, disappointment, fear of abandonment, helplessness. Of necessity, you become egocentric, for it is you who must sort out what needs to be done. Some friends become closer; others let you down. Although you may have told yourself and others that you are most concerned about the children, you may very well have forgotten about communicating with them at this crucial time.

Let's assume that you have decided to engage in a custody dispute. Your four-year-old child already knows something is very wrong because Daddy doesn't live at home any more. He sees his father at different times and is never sure just when these times will be. And he sees you upset a great deal—perhaps even in tears. You have finally found the courage to tell your son that you and his father will no longer live together. Perhaps you've even used the word "divorce." Four-year-olds certainly know that word. But now comes the custody suit. Do you tell your child about it?

You must. Even a four-year-old should know if there is going to be a custody dispute. Once it appears certain, it is time to let your child know about it. You must tell him because he will learn about it anyway, and may have very frightening fantasies about what it means. You need not go into all the details, of course, but any attempts at subterfuge may well create even more stress for the child than the dispute itself.

The Gibson family was being interviewed by Dr. Barash, the child psychiatrist appointed by the court to perform a custody evaluation. There were two children: Arlen, four, and Ethan, six. The doctor was about to begin the first session—with Arlen and Ethan together—when Mrs. Gibson edged her way into the office ahead of her sons.

"I need to speak with you for a minute!" she whispered.

Dr. Barash replied that this was really a time set aside for the children, and that they could talk during her own scheduled sessions with him.

"I know that," she said, "but I have to speak with you now."

The boys looked at both the doctor and their mother and then began to play with some toys in the waiting room. Mrs. Gibson did not wait for the doctor's assent; she closed the office door behind her.

"Just one thing," she said. "Please don't discuss our custody fight with Arlen and Ethan. They don't know anything about it, and I don't want to get them upset."

"I can just about promise you," said Dr. Barash, "that they both know what's going on. Most children in this situation do. I do need to find out certain things from them, but I promise you that I'll be gentle with them."

Mrs. Gibson left the office, saying to her boys, "Okay, fellas. The doctor just wants to play and talk with you for a while. Mommy will be right out here in the waiting room."

Dr. Barash sat down at the lay table with Arlen and Ethan. They all began to color. In a little while, after some idle chatter, Dr. Barash asked, "Do you kids know why you're here?"

Ethan, the six-year-old, said: "Yeah, because our parents fight a lot. They scream, too."

"What do you think I can do about it?" asked Dr. Barash.

"My daddy said that you will talk to the judge," Ethan went on. "You can tell the judge to make them stop fighting."

"What are they fighting about?"

Ethan didn't answer. Instead, he suddenly became very engrossed in his coloring. It was Arlen, the four-year-old, who supplied the answer.

"They're fighting about us. My daddy wants us to live with him and my mommy wants us to live with her. All the time they're fighting about this. Once I thought my father was going to hit my mommy, but he didn't. I was so scared. They yell so loud."

"What do you do when they yell so loud?" asked Dr. Barash.

"I hide in my room and cry."

Psychiatrist and children went on to discuss the custody dispute. Ethan talked about not knowing what to do. Although Dr. Barash never asked the boys where they wanted to live, they both said they wanted to live with both parents. Arlen said that he wasn't able to decide where to live, but he knew he wanted to stay with his brother.

One reason why it is so important to acknowledge the custody dispute with your children is that telling them about it validates their own feelings and perceptions. When children become aware of something in themselves or their environment and parents contradict them—even with the best of intentions —it confuses children and leads them to mistrust their own senses. When a young child sees a parent upset, for example, she might ask: "Mommy, are you sad? Why are you so un-happy?" If the mother then replies, "I'm not sad; everything is fine," the child will become confused. Knowing that their in-tuitions are correct helps children become more self-confident and independent. So even if you and the other parent are not on the best of terms, it is extremely important for you to call a truce long enough to agree on a way to discuss the dispute with your child and avoid placing her in the middle of your dispute.

The Slaters were disputing the custody of their five-year-old daughter, Jenny. Mrs. Slater lived in the city. Mr. Slater had just moved to a house in the suburbs and hoped to have Jenny living there with him soon. Mrs. Slater had recently purchased a puppy for Jenny to help make up for the turmoil over the breakup of the marriage. When Jenny was spending time with her father, he would often say to her: "You know, your puppy could already be housebroken if you lived with me in this big house, instead of with your mother in the city," or "It's cruel to keep a puppy shut up all day in an apartment."

During an evaluation session with a child psychiatrist, Jenny said: "I want to live with my daddy. I hate the city. It's so dirty. My dog can't run around." Yet in another session just a few days later, she said, "I don't know where I want to live."

If each parent could have evaluated Jenny's feelings outside the arena of the custody battle, they would have understood how important it is not to carry on such a dispute through the child. But at this point, parents are often so angry at each other that they involve the child in ways that can only cause anxiety and confusion. By now, you know you need to proceed differ-ently. Now is the time for both of you to try to agree on how to inform your child about what lies ahead.

□ TELL THE TRUTH—BUT □
CONSIDER THE CHILD'S AGE

How you tell your child is as important as what you say. For example, a four-year-old can be told something like this: "Mommy and Daddy are having an argument about which of us is going to live with you. We both love you very much and no matter what happens, we're always going to love you and take care of you. But if we can't decide ourselves what to do, the judge will have to do it." Even four-year-olds have some concept of a judge and will usually understand that someone else will make the decision. An older child of, say, seven, can be told a bit more: by that age, a child probably has friends whose parents have been through a divorce and possibly even a custody dispute. (It would help if you can find out about this, so that you can get a sense of what your child is experiencing.) A seven-year-old knows something about disputes and resolutions, has a better sense of what a judge is, and will probably have more questions for you. Be prepared for them. The child will probably be glad to have permission to ask.

A seven-year-old might ask, "Where will I live?" You can answer that it is undecided at present. Some children—even those as young as seven—ask to speak or write to the judge. Children of this age are just learning about rules and regulations, what is fair and what isn't, and what cheating is about. The judge embodies fairness. If your child wants to contact the judge, by all means encourage her to do so.

Seven-year-old Allison wrote to the judge telling him how she often felt caught in the middle of her parents' constant arguments. She spent a long time on the letter and used her best penmanship. She saw the judge as an adult who would know what was fair and right, as someone who would make her parents do the right thing. Allison asked her mother for the judge's address and was given it. This particular mother did not ask Allison to show her the letter first; she respected her daughter's right to privacy. The judge received the letter and with Allison's permission, he allowed both parents to read it. For the first time, Allison's mother and father were able to see the emotional fallout of their custody battle, and this prompted the beginning of negotiations toward a resolution of their dispute.

A seven-year-old's preoccupation with fairness makes her especially vulnerable to feeling treated unjustly. Indeed, you yourself may feel the same way. Perhaps you feel that the financial arrangements are unfair, or that the lawyers are taking advantage of you, or that your spouse has reneged on some previous agreements. It would be so easy to ally yourself with the child at this point. The two of you could cry "Unfair!" and unite against the other parent. It is a temptation that must be resisted.

Adele, age seven, lived with her mother. Her father, an investment banker, had a great deal more money than his ex-wife, who was a schoolteacher, and he socialized with the rich and famous in his city. Adele's mother resented this disparity and never let Adele forget how difficult it was for her to make ends meet. She told Adele that summer camp was out of the question, unless her father agreed to pay. The same thing was true for piano lessons. The usual scenario went like this: Adele would tell her mother that she needed a certain amount of money for a special event on a future weekend. Her mother would reply, "I can't pay for it, Adele. Call your father, although I know what the answer will be." The seven-year-old would call. Sometimes her father said yes; other times he said no. When he did say no, Adele's mother would say, "See? I told you. He's so unfair! He's making us suffer. If you talk to the judge, you can tell her that, Adele." When her father said yes to Adele, her mother would say, "He must have something up his sleeve. His lawyer probably told him to give you the money now, and then he's going to take it out on me later. He's a liar."

While you may be tempted to team up with your child against the other parent, do your best not to, in order to spare your child the certain results of such behavior. In exchange for possibly making yourself feel a bit more in control and power-ful, you will be causing your child a great deal of anxiety. Remind yourself that the custody dispute is between you and the other parent; it does not involve the team of you and your child versus the other parent. The sooner you accept this fact, the better it will be for you and your child.

Children in the preteen and early teenage years often react to news of a custody dispute with anger and resentment. One misconception about kids of this age is that they are so involved with themselves and their friends that they don't care much about their own family. Parents often interpret a teenager's reluctance to spend time with the family as lack of interest, or see it as a sign of the child's definitive cutting of the umbilical cord. In fact, children in this age group do care a great deal about what goes on at home, and their relationships with their parents are extremely important to them. They depend on emotional support from the family to fuel their ability to en-gage in activities outside the home. And even as these young people criticize their parents or get into fights with them, their mothers and fathers are central figures in their lives.

Thus, a custody dispute involving a preteen or a young teen-ager will have as profound an emotional impact on the child as it does on younger children. A twelve-year-old child will often become angry upon hearing the news, and may bombard you with all kinds of questions in an attempt to make sense of this extremely complicated situation. A child who has become used to serving as a mediator between two squabbling parents may try to settle this dispute as well.

Janie Becker, twelve, had just learned about her parents' cus-tody battle. Her mother had told her about it while her father was out of town on a business trip. Mrs. Becker had broken the news in a way that portrayed her as the only loving, caring parent, and depicted her husband as an ineffectual, uninvolved father. Janie did not believe this herself, but she did not know what to say to her mother. Nevertheless, she wanted to inter-vene and settle the dispute. Some time afterward, Janie was talking on the telephone with her father; her mother was whispering in her ear and trying to influence her about what to say. Mr. Becker, realizing this, demanded to speak to the mother, and the two parents got into a heated exchange. Janie tried to calm them down, but her efforts were fruitless. She ended up screaming at both of them. She slammed down the telephone and ran crying to her room. As the weeks passed, she continued to try to mediate, and this took its toll: Janie developed severe abdominal pain for which her doctor was unable to find any physical explanation.

It is important to explain the situation to preteens and teenagers in a way that avoids drawing them into the conflict. Focus on the fact that this is an issue between you and your spouse, that it has to do with your own views on parenting, and that you have honest differences about your roles. Stress that the two of you will attempt to work things out, but that a judge might have to make the final decision. Make it clear that you both can handle this delicate problem and do not "fish" for support from your child.

Depending on the particular family circumstances, older children can also be particularly quick to develop alliances with one parent. These alliances may grow out of their living arrangement at the time, or out of their need to identify with one parent over another; they may be fostered, consciously or not, by a parent.

Ted Hoffmann was twelve and lived with his mother after his father moved out. When he learned that his parents were going to add a custody dispute to their divorce proceedings, he became very angry at his mother. He made it clear to her that he wanted to live with his father, and even threatened to run away from home to be with him, although Mr. Hoffman lived in another town. Ted's father supported his son. He told Ted that his mother had lied in the papers she and her lawyer had submitted to the judge; he also said that she had always tried to exclude him from Ted's life. Ted, in turn, told the evaluating psychiatrist that his mother was a liar, that she punished him excessively, that she was lazy (unlike his father), and that he hated being with her. Whenever he was scheduled to spend the weekend with his mother, he would announce that he wanted to be with his father instead.

This all made for a pretty convincing case . . . on the surface. But there are always two sides to such a situation, and no professional would take these positions at face value.

Talking to an older child about a custody battle requires a great deal of sensitivity, particularly when the child is articulate, aware, and even somewhat psychologically sophisticated, as many children of Ted's age are. You might assume that because your child is intelligent and sensitive, you can divulge a great many details about the dispute and share your own feelings as well. Referring to her thirteen-year-old daughter, one mother often said, "We're really good pals—best friends. I can tell Elyse anything, and she'll understand me." Elyse *was* bright and sensitive—but she was also only thirteen. Regardless of her mother's perceptions, she had a lot more growing up to do before she could really understand and assimilate what her mother was saying. Elyse was being forced to become an adult too quickly in order to satisfy her mother's own needs.

Divorcing parents often turn to their children for support and affection when they feel needy and insecure about themselves. On the surface, this seems a natural phenomenon. Yet what sometimes happens in these situations is that children are inappropriately placed in the role of confidant. In these cases, parents may begin to tell children deeply personal things, to complain about the other parent, or even ask a child's advice about what to do next. Sometimes children rise to the occasion, seeming to help a parent through these difficult times. In other instances, children resist this pressure and rebel in various ways. Neither reaction is particularly desirable.

So don't give in to the urge to unburden yourself to your child, even if she seems to be inviting you to open up. It is simply not fair to the child. No matter how proud you are of her intelligence and insight, your daughter will not be able to fill the role of "best friend" for you without suffering emotionally. Seek solace elsewhere. If you need to, seek professional help or confide in an adult friend or a trusted relative. Do not ask your child to perform this function. If you are even now telling yourself "But my child is different!" then think again; there are no exceptions.

What you *can* tell an older child is that you and the other parent have tried—and will still try—to reach an agreement, but that you have differing views about her custody. You can say that you are extremely sorry this has happened and that it hurts you and even angers you at times, so you can imagine how she might be feeling. After you have said this as directly as possible, you can encourage your child to talk about how she feels. Even without prompting, she will probably take sides and identify one parent as the good one and the other as the bad. You will be doing your child a great service if you can avoid playing into this kind of discussion. Ideally, you should say something like, "I know it's easy to blame somebody in this and to take sides. It even helps deal with the pain for a while. But I don't think it really solves the problem—and it only takes away the hurt for a little while. We both love you a great deal."

REMEMBER AGAIN THAT children will react to news about a custody dispute according to their stage of development. A young child will think in terms of loss and abandonment. Even as you explain that his parents disagree about who will live with him, be sure to make it clear repeatedly that the child will not be deserted, and that both of you will be very much involved in his life. Saying the words will not be enough; you will have to support them with behavior. If you are furious with the other parent for a variety of reasons, you may try to restrict your child's access to that parent; if you do, his natural fears of abandonment will be intensified and will seem to be based on reality, despite your assurances to the contrary.

As the custody dispute progresses, keep your young child informed as much as possible. You can explain to a child of four, five, or six that you and the other parent will be asking the judge to decide with which parent he will live. You can review facts that the child should already know: that you and the other parent cannot agree on where he will live, and that this is why the judge is going to help. Even if your child does not ask any questions, he will be aware that you are going to court, so don't assume he is not interested. He may be afraid to say anything for fear of making you angry or worried. You can explore this with him and give him permission to ask you questions.

Later chapters focus on how to prepare your child for a possible psychiatric evaluation, for your day in court, and how to deal with the judicial decision. But throughout the entire process, the key for the young child is to feel secure and taken care of, and to know that both parents love him very much, even if they are not able to love each other.

A child of seven or eight will want to know more particulars —for example, whether or not you and the other parent are being treated fairly by the judge and by each other. You can tell her some details about lawyers and the role of the judge, and that judges work very hard to see that childrens' best interests are looked after. You can even say that the judge might want to talk to her during the course of the proceedings. But do not involve children in the legal strategies or discuss why you are still angry at the other parent or lawyer.

If your child should express a desire to write to the judge, don't discourage her. You might want to ask what she wants to say and what she hopes will come of it. If the child agrees to discuss this with you, the communication can be helpful for both of you. If not, respect that decision, and don't press. If your child asks "What will the judge decide?" answer honestly that you do not know, but that you will tell her when the judge tells you.

It's likely that your preteen or teenage child will want to be kept well informed about the dispute. You should provide some information, but beware of trying to make a pal or ally out of an older child by confiding all the details of the case and all your feelings. It is self-serving to do this and as we have noted before, potentially damaging to the child. She can be told about court dates, evaluations, and so on, but need not be flooded with everything you know, as if she were your best friend.

In all cases and for all ages, keep in mind that no matter how angry you are, and no matter what you think of your soon-to-be ex-wife or ex-husband, your children will never feel the same way. Their relationship with their father or mother was —and always will be—quite different from yours. If you launch a campaign to try to convince them that you are the best parent in the world and that they do not need the other parent, you will only confuse and hurt them and add to their anxiety.

It is sometimes surprisingly difficult for parents to be honest with their children. In the long run, however, making up little lies (and big ones) does them a great disservice and interferes with the parent-child relationship. It is the truth, rendered with discretion and respect for childrens' abilities to assimilate it, that can act as a salve for the pain they feel at this unhappy time in their lives.

BUILDING YOUR CASE

IN ADDITION TO all the other stresses of the divorce, you are now dealing with another uncomfortable reality: a great many people you hardly know are becoming involved in your personal life. It was probably a bit strange the first time you discussed your divorce problems with a lawyer, for you found yourself revealing extremely personal information—about your past, about your marital history, even intimate details about your sex life. Your lawyer should have explained the reasons for eliciting this information from you and should conduct the interviews in a respectful and professional manner.

If there is a custody dispute, still more areas of your private life may become public. You will be asked by your lawyer to review the history of your relationship with your children: what you did with them and how you did it, your feelings about parenthood, your hopes and dreams for them, and so on. In addition, your lawyer will want you to come up with reasons why you would be the better parent. In order to have the ammunition she thinks is needed to win your case, your lawyer may ask you to think of specific examples that cast the other parent in a poor light and allow you to shine: a time when the other parent struck the child, examples of low moral behavior that would adversely affect the well-being of a child, an occasion when the child did not want to be with the other parent and preferred to be with you, a time when the other parent seemed irresponsible. Unfortunately, some lawyers encourage clients to embellish and exaggerate these charges to make a good argument. This is never a good idea and will only escalate the conflict. Now is also the time when allegations of physical or sexual abuse committed against the child may surface. (See chapter 8 for further discussion of this topic.) Given what you now know about how children experience custody disputes, you will have to work very hard at remaining in control of your case and at protecting your children.

□ REVIEWING YOUR TROOPS □

Your lawyer may suggest that other people become involved in your custody dispute: your child's pediatrician and dentist, teachers, and even, if appropriate, babysitters and neighbors. They may be used by your lawyer as "witnesses of fact," that is, as people who have specific, firsthand information about the situation. These witnesses may be called upon to make a deposition on your behalf or to testify in court. (A deposition is an examination before trial in which witnesses are questioned by lawyers for both sides. The entire transcript of these interviews becomes available to both sides and may become part of each side's strategy.) Your lawyer's purpose in enlisting these people is to prove that you are indeed the excellent parent you say you are. For example, a psychotherapist, should you have one, will be expected to know you very well and to be able to supply good clinical data in support of your parenting abilities. Should your child have a therapist, he or she would also be counted on to know what is best for your child and what kind of parent you have been. Teachers will certainly know just how involved you have been in your child's school. Babysitters, mother's helpers, and neighbors might all provide basic information about you and your daily life that could convince a judge of your worthiness as a parent.

But although these people may enhance your position, their involvement can be fraught with complications and may even backfire. Let's look at what could happen if, for instance, your therapist is brought in.

Susan Halloman had been in therapy twice a week for about a year with Dr. Alan Feld, a psychologist. As part of the custody dispute, her husband, Jerry, was charging that because of her frequent bouts of depression, she was an unfit parent for their four-year-old daughter, Ellen. Susan had first gone to see Dr. Feld while in a moderate depression. She had recovered and had not needed antidepressant medication.

Susan's lawyer suggested that a letter from Dr. Feld to the court would be very helpful to her case. Dr. Feld should certainly be the one to comment upon her emotional state, and a clean bill of health from him would go a long way toward offsetting her husband's charges that she was psychologically unfit to care for the child. Dr. Feld agreed to write a letter on behalf of his patient. This is the letter he sent to the judge:

To Whom it May Concern:

I have been treating Susan Halloman, a thirty-one-year-old junior high school mathematics teacher, twice a week with cognitive and behavioral therapy for depression since April 3, 1985. Four months after beginning treatment with me, her depression had abated significantly. However, after two more months of treatment, she suffered a relapse. I was about to refer her for medication consultation with Dr. Henry Saslow, a psychiatrist. However, she began to improve again and did not require antidepressant medication.

From time to time during her treatment, Mrs. Halloman has spoken about her daughter, Ellen, with a great deal of affection. She has described their "private time" together in the evenings, when they sit by the fire and read to each other. She has talked of how much Ellen loves Mrs. Halloman's parents and how they sometimes go on weekend trips to the Adirondack Mountains, where they stay in her grandparents' cabin. Ellen loves to go fishing with her mother and grandfather and also loves cooking with her grandmother. Mrs. Halloman is quite devoted to her daughter and most concerned about her welfare.

Three months ago, Mrs. Halloman came into my office with her left arm in a sling. She said her husband had twisted it the night before and she was in a great deal of pain.

Two months ago Mr. Halloman requested a joint meeting with his wife to discuss the impending divorce and its effects upon their daughter. When I suggested that such a meeting might make Mrs. Hallowman uncomfortable, he cursed at me and hung up.

In my opinion, Susan Halloman has been an excellent mother in spite of her marital difficulties.

Sincerely,
Alan Feld, Ph.D.

On first reading, this letter may seem helpful, but let's look a bit more closely and see how and why it actually complicated things for Susan. First, the letter states that Susan had had a depression that abated, and that she had always been a devoted and concerned mother. But as the lawyer for the other side pointed out, Dr. Feld's knowledge was limited.

Waving the letter, the lawyer asked, "Excuse me, Dr. Feld, but on what information did you base your conclusion that Susan Halloman is such a devoted mother? Have you ever met Ellen, her daughter?" ("No.") "Have you ever seen Susan Halloman with Ellen?" ("No.") "Have you ever observed Susan Halloman performing any so-called maternal tasks with her daughter?" ("No, I haven't.") "Do you have any information from outside sources about the history of Susan Halloman's relationship with her daughter, Ellen?" ("No, I do not.") "Then, Dr. Feld, what you are telling us today is that everything you know about Mrs. Halloman's parenting abilities and her relationship with her daughter, and everything you wrote about that in this letter, is based solely upon what Susan Halloman told you herself, and nothing else?" ("Yes.")

Poor Dr. Feld. He was extremely uncomfortable by now, but the lawyer was not finished with him. Next, he was asked why he had included two seemingly unrelated paragraphs in the letter. The first contained the statements about the arm in a sling, and the second, the information about Mr. Halloman cursing and hanging up on him. Dr. Feld was asked whether he believed his patient when she told him that her husband had inflicted the injury—a lose-lose situation both for the psychologist and for Susan. If Dr. Feld said yes, he believed her, he could be portrayed as gullible and biased. The lawyer could depict him as a "hired gun," brought in only to make the other side look bad. If, on the other hand, Dr. Feld answered that he was not sure if Jerry Halloman had twisted the arm—an answer that would be certain to upset Susan—he would be asked why he had included that information in his letter in the first place.

Dr. Feld replied, "At the time, I believed that Susan had been hurt by her husband and that he had shown little interest in her welfare. Now I realize that I had very little information to go on. I guess I should just be a psychologist and not try to be a detective."

The second paragraph under challenge had to do with Mr. Halloman's hanging up. What, Mr. Halloman's lawyer asked, did Dr. Feld mean by including that?

"Did you conclude, Dr. Feld, that Mr. Halloman was not concerned for his daughter's welfare after all?" ("No, not necessarily.") "Well, then, why include it except to inflame the situation further and to make Ellen's father appear to be angry and irrational? Could there have been other reasons for Mr. Halloman to hang up?" ("Certainly.") "Might he have legitimately felt a bit uneasy with your response?" ("Yes, that's possible.") "And wasn't it quite responsible of Mr. Halloman to call you in the first place? Wasn't that responsible of him?" ("Yes, I guess it was.") "You *guess* it was, Dr. Feld? You mean you're not sure?" ("It was responsible.")

Dr. Feld probably wished he were safely ensconced in his own office at this point. But Mr. Halloman's lawyer was cruising at high speed. She asked him about the last paragraph of his letter, in which he stated that Susan Halloman was an "excellent mother." She asked Dr. Feld what "excellent" meant in this context, and on what grounds he had chosen that particular phrase. What were Dr. Feld's credentials, the lawyer asked rather pointedly. Had he conducted a child custody evaluation according to the accepted standards of the profession? ("No.") Therefore, in a triumphant climax that entirely demolished Dr. Feld's by-now shaky credibility, Jerry Halloman's lawyer suggested that his conclusions here were based not on sound psychological principles but rather upon hearsay.

By the time Dr. Feld stepped down from the witness stand, Susan's case had taken a turn for the worse. Certainly, much of his testimony had been discredited. Moreover, a great deal of damage had been done to the therapist-patient relationship. By involving Dr. Feld directly in the custody dispute, Susan and her lawyer had turned the psychologist into a forensic, or legal, witness, and had in essence waived the normal rules of therapist-patient confidentiality. Dr. Feld left the courtroom feeling upset and angry at both Susan and himself for having become involved in the proceedings. And Susan was disappointed in his courtroom "performance." A great deal of work would be required before Dr. Feld and Susan could resume their normal relationship.

Introducing such a letter and such testimony might have turned out better in another courtroom or with other lawyers. The point is that in Susan's case it did not, and that this is the kind of outcome you risk when you proceed as Susan did. The important lesson to remember is that in general, no matter what your lawyer may say, leave your therapist out of your custody dispute!

Therapy can serve as a source of strength and security when you are particularly stressed. Precisely because of this, your therapist should not be directly involved in your legal problems and should not write letters for you, talk to your lawyer, or testify in court. If your lawyer wants to present a psychiatric evaluation of you, another therapist should be engaged to do it; your therapist is not an impartial, court-appointed expert and can never be regarded as objective. If necessary, the outside mental health professional can consult with your therapist.

What about your child's therapist? Should he participate in your custody case? In some ways, he might seem like the ideal witness. After all, who else besides you knows your child's mind so well? Who else can interpret so accurately her deepest feelings about the divorce and custody battle? And who better to tell the judge your child's true preferences? The temptation to enlist this person might be even greater than the desire to involve your own therapist.

Resist it. Although it's true that the few visits the court-appointed expert has with your child pale in comparison with the multitude of opportunities for observation that her own therapist has had, it will be far wiser to leave him out of the custody dispute. Your child's visits to a therapist are just as private as your own—and you (and your lawyer) should respect that privacy. Remember, the client is you, not your child, and that is why you must be her advocate now and work to protect her from being used as a tool in your behalf.

Gus and Marie DiNardo had been married for ten years. Their eleven-year-old daughter, Felicia, had been in therapy for the past two years with Dr. Angela Thomas, a child and adolescent psychiatrist. Mr. DiNardo was convinced that his wife's admitted affair with a married man, as well as her habit of taking off for points unknown for days at a time, were actions detrimental to Felicia's well-being.

Felicia had been considered a behavior problem in school since third grade. She hardly ever participated in classwork, always talked out of turn, could never hold a pencil or a crayon properly, and seemed to be exceptionally moody. After extensive psychological testing, Felicia was found to have a learning disability. It was the evaluating psychologist's opinion that in addition to specialized educational programs, Felicia ought to be in therapy to help her deal with the emotional consequences of the learning disorder.

Initially resistant to the idea of going to the child psychiatrist, Felicia eventually developed a very close and warm therapeutic relationship with Dr. Thomas. She came to trust the doctor, and over time her behavior problems abated. She made wonderful progress in school as well. After she became aware of the divorce and custody dispute, Felicia treated her therapy sessions as a refuge from the tension and anxiety she felt at home. With Dr. Thomas, she could be herself and could talk freely about how she felt. Without her therapy, Felicia might well have relapsed into her earlier behavior patterns.

Felicia's parents were highly supportive of their daughter's continuing treatment with Dr. Thomas, and Mr. DiNardo was very willing to pay for the visits. But his lawyer believed that Dr. Thomas could serve another purpose: she could tell the court how Felicia was suffering because of the divorce and custody proceedings. In particular, the lawyer maintained, the judge would recognize the negative impact on the child of her mother's unexplained disappearances and her supposed involvement with other men. According to Mr. DiNardo's lawyer, Dr. Thomas would be just the kind of witness to impress the judge. He would not ask her to offer an opinion on custody, the lawyer said, because he knew that she had not performed a formal child custody evaluation. But he was certain that Dr. Thomas could provide tremendous insight into Felicia's mind and could help convince the judge that she belonged with her father.

Again, this kind of legal advice, while it might indeed be helpful for the client, could very well be harmful for the child. Involving a child's therapist in this way contaminates the therapeutic relationship. Once Dr. Thomas became a witness for the court, her function as Felicia's therapist would be compromised. She would be drawn into the legal aspects of the dispute, instead of remaining a neutral base of support for Felicia.

In this case, Dr. Thomas had the experience to tell the father's lawyer that she did not wish to become involved and would neither provide a letter nor testify. The lawyer nevertheless had a subpoena issued for her, thus forcing Dr. Thomas to come to court on the first day of the custody hearing. She was very angry, but she was now legally bound to appear. Fortunately, the judge in this case was both sensitive and psychologically aware. She asked Mr. DiNardo's lawyer why he had forced Dr. Thomas to appear. He replied that as the child's therapist, she had a great deal to contribute to the case.

At that point, the judge turned to Dr. Wilfred Hawkins, the court-appointed impartial expert, who had conducted a full custody evaluation on Felicia and her family. When the judge asked Dr. Hawkins if he thought Dr. Thomas's testimony was crucial to the case, Dr. Hawkins replied that it was not. He informed the judge that he had spoken with Dr. Thomas over the telephone and could relay some of her concerns to the court. Dr. Hawkins also told the judge he thought it would be detrimental to the child's relationship with her therapist to demand that Dr. Thomas participate in the court proceedings.

The judge sent Dr. Thomas home, saying, "It's Doctor Hawkins I want to hear from. He's the only one who has seen everyone in the family and has been objective and impartial from the start. And he's spoken to Dr. Thomas as part of his own evaluation of this family, so his testimony is the important part of this case." Mr. DiNardo did obtain custody of his daughter anyway. With the complete evaluation of the court-appointed expert, it was not necessary for Felicia's therapist to be in court.

Remember, you can always have the court-appointed expert contact the child's therapist for general comments about your child's emotional state. But keep the therapeutic relationship separate from the custody dispute. Give your child freedom to use therapy for growth and development and as a refuge from intense family tensions and anxieties.

Your child's teacher may be another person brought into the custody dispute. Typically, teachers are asked by one party or the other to offer a letter or testimony not so much to describe the status of the child in school as to offer their observations of your parenting. For example, a father may insist that he has been the parent who brought his four-year-son to nursery school every morning, not the mother. The mother may challenge this assertion and in fact, charge that the father never showed any interest in his son's school life. A letter from the child's teacher could help to clarify which parent was doing what.

As a "witness of fact," the teacher could legitimately write a truthful, straightforward letter or affidavit that would simply summarize what she knew. Such a letter might look like this:

Hon. Kathleen O'Hara, Justice
Supreme Court
45 Elm Street
Grove City, Maine 01888

Dear Judge O'Hara:

I have known Jimmy Rizzo for the past nine months, as his primary nursery school teacher. Jimmy attended school regularly for the morning session during the 1988–89 school year. Throughout that year, Jimmy was brought to school primarily by his father.

Occasionally, perhaps once every two to three weeks, Mrs. Rizzo brought her son in. In general, however, Mr. Rizzo brought Jimmy and would often stay for ten or fifteen minutes until Jimmy settled down.

In addition, Mr. Rizzo participated in all school functions involving parents and attended all four parent-teacher conferences held throughout that year.

> *Sincerely,*
> *Valerie LaRoche,*
> *Teacher*
> *Happy Rabbit*
> *Nursery School*

This letter is appropriate because it simply states a series of facts. It does not gush in praise of Mr. Rizzo, nor does it imply that Mrs. Rizzo does not take proper care of her son. It provides objective data in support of the father's contention that he has indeed been very much involved in his child's life at school.

This letter is acceptable and useful. Teachers are on slippery ground, however, when they offer opinions about parental fitness, or even about the custody dispute itself. If you are planning to request help from a child's teacher, limit your request to *facts* about you and your child that she would know. Resist the impulse to enlist her help in convincing the judge that you are a better, more involved, and more responsible parent. Such a limitation, while perhaps frustrating for you, will do your child a real service in the long run. It keeps the teacher from having to enter into unpleasant personal family affairs and allows her to remain an impartial support for the child. It also allows the teacher to do what she does best, which is teach.

Another outside person who may be drawn into a custody dispute is the child's pediatrician. With the national divorce rate at around 50 percent, more and more pediatricians are encountering divorce in the families of their young patients. Sometimes divorcing parents are honest with their children's doctors and inform them early on, so that they can be alert to the child's emotional state during this difficult time. Other parents are reluctant to discuss their private affairs with their pediatrician. Still, these doctors are often the first to pick up signs of a young patient's behavioral disturbance, and worried parents often consult a pediatrician before going to a child psychologist or psychiatrist.

But although pediatricians are experts in children's health and may be of great help in identifying what's troubling your child, they often find themselves used in all kinds of unhelpful ways by parents engaged in a custody dispute. Sometimes a parent will make the child's health an issue in the dispute, claiming that he is the parent who is more concerned with and more knowledgeable about the child's well-being. One particular father was convinced that his soon-to-be ex-wife was not feeding their seven-year-old son properly. He considered the boy to be too thin, "on the way to being anorexic." Whenever he had the child for a visit, he would take him to one pediatrician after another. He kept a dossier on his child's health and filled it with weight and height measurements as well as reports from several of the pediatricians who examined the child. Occasionally, a doctor would note that the boy was "too thin," although no doctor ever said the child was malnourished. The mother in turn obtained several letters from *her* pediatrician, as well as from a registered dietician, all attesting to her ability to feed her son properly.

In fact the boy *was* thin, but so were both parents, and the child himself did not like rich foods. The boy's meals with his father became power struggles, with the child resisting the father's attempts to make him eat various foods. At one point, he began to vomit whenever he ate with his father. This behavior eventually abated, but the child's anxiety level was still high —and the constant doctor's appointments only made him even more nervous and unhappy.

In another case, a father claimed that his ex-wife was denying him visitation with his eleven-year-old son. Whenever she told him the child was sick and therefore couldn't visit, this man became angry and verbally abusive. On one occasion, he actually convinced a pediatrician to make a home visit to examine the child and verify that he was indeed ill. The father accompanied the doctor to the house. Literally over the child's bed, he and the mother engaged in a bitter argument while the pediatrician was doing a physical examination. The child *was* ill, with a high fever and a bad sore throat. The pediatrician later said that she had felt quite foolish making that house call and resented being used in that way. She also expressed concern that this completely unnecessary visit might have upset the child psychologically.

Now, as with the teacher, it is perfectly appropriate for the doctor to write a letter on your behalf, stating that you brought your child for visits, listened, asked questions, seemed involved, called when the child was ill or might have been ill, and so on. If there is an allegation of physical or sexual abuse, certainly the pediatrician might inform the court about any physical evidence, or indicate the lack therof. (An independent physician trained to detect physical or sexual abuse is often brought in as a consultant on such cases.) However, the pediatrician should *not* be involved in making judgments about parenting styles, who seemed to care the most, or who would make the better parent. Your child's physician has no expertise in formulating opinions about custody. He or she did not conduct—and is not trained to conduct—a full-fledged child custody evaluation. Do not ask this doctor to become involved in your cause in any way other than as the physician of record for your child.

If, in your custody dispute, there is a health issue in which some major disagreement exists between you and the other parent—whether tonsils should be removed or a certain asthma medicine prescribed—you may want to consider engaging an outside pediatrician to act as a consultant. This person, paid by both sides, could get access to any pertinent medical records, could examine your child, and then write a report for the court and put the health matter to rest. Do not shop around for pediatricians to examine your child. Consider the effect upon your child of being subjected to exam after exam, poked at and palpated. Think about how you would feel if this happened to you. Not only would you find it extremely unpleasant, but it could make you frightened, angry, resentful, and insecure. A child, armed with fewer defenses than you, will almost certainly find it even more distressing.

Another person who might be drawn into the custody process is your child's babysitter or nanny, if you have one. It is common for a parent to ask a babysitter to make a written or oral statement about one parent's fitness and the other's unfitness. Sometimes, when a family is being evaluated by a court-appointed psychiatrist, one parent may request that he interview the babysitter or read that person's statement. But, the use of a babysitter or nanny as a character witness for one parent is considered of limited value by the court-appointed evaluator. Babysitters are usually perceived as allied with one side—they are often accused by one parent of lying, or even of having an affair with the other—and therefore, not the best sources of objective data. The same can be said of a neighbor (who most likely will not have all the facts either, but may be all too ready with an opinion), and other family members.

Unfortunately, professionals and nonprofessionals alike are all too frequently asked to participate in custody disputes that go beyond their knowledge or expertise. The inappropriate use of others to bolster your position can backfire and in some cases, even harm your child. In general, if you ask others to make written or oral statements on your behalf, limit your request to facts that confirm some of your arguments. Even if —in moments of desperation—you are tempted to enlist the help of anyone and everyone who knows something about you and your child, try to remember that in this case, less is more.

THE EXPERT
WITNESS

7

A CUSTODY DISPUTE can make you feel control is slipping away from you. This is *your* life and *your* child, but soon a band of outside players enters the picture: lawyers and, especially, "experts." Don't assume that just because they are billed as experts, you can entrust them with full responsibility for your case. You'll still have your work cut out for you making sure that these people are competent and ethical, and what is foremost in their minds—as in yours—is the best interest of your child.

With court calendars becoming increasingly crowded, judges making custody decisions rely heavily on the opinions of expert witnesses. Just what *is* an expert witness? From a legal perspective, it is simply someone who, on the basis of special knowledge, education, or professional experience, is asked by the court—or by one of the litigants—to offer an *opinion* on a case.

Unfortunately, U.S. law provides no criteria for the qualifications of expert witnesses in custody disputes, and judges themselves are not always well informed. In a custody case in New York State a few years ago, for example, the supreme court judge allowed a young psychiatrist to testify as an expert witness. This particular "expert" had very little training and even less actual experience in working with children, nor had he received any special training in custody evaluation. Nevertheless, the judge gave special weight to his testimony in the custody decision.

□ WHO IS AN EXPERT WITNESS? □

In a child custody dispute, the expert witness is a mental health professional, usually a child psychiatrist or psychologist. General psychiatrists, while not trained as child psychiatrists, may be called upon to perform evaluations, and some regions also recognize psychiatric social workers as experts.

A psychiatrist is a medical doctor with four additional years of postgraduate training in psychiatry. However, you should know that psychiatrists who are not fully trained *child* psychiatrists may have had very little training or experience working with children. A child psychiatrist is a medical doctor whose postgraduate training includes three or four years of psychiatry plus two years of child psychiatry. This education may or may not have included formal training in child custody evaluation. Only a few medical centers in the United States routinely offer classes in custody evaluation. (These include the Yale Child Study Center, the University of Michigan, and Columbia University.) Other programs may expose trainees to no more than five hours of study in medical-legal issues—of which child custody is but one aspect—during the two years of specialized training.

Psychologists who perform custody evaluations usually have a doctorate in clinical psychology; they will also have experience conducting psychotherapy with adults and depending upon the postgraduate program, with children as well.

Psychiatric social workers usually have a master's degree in social work (M.S.W.), with special training in working with the mentally ill. But they usually have received less education in the area of child psychology than psychiatrists and psychologists, unless they have taken extra courses or requested extra supervision on their own initiative. Because social workers often work at community agencies, they are frequently called upon by the courts to evaluate custody disputes, even though —with some major exceptions—few have actually received specific training in this field.

LET'S LOOK AT the ways expert witnesses become involved in a custody dispute, and what your participation should be if one is suggested for your situation. At the start of a case, the judge will often ask the lawyers to agree on a court-appointed expert witness. But beware! As we have observed, just because the judge recommends someone and the lawyers agree, it doesn't necessarily follow that the expert is highly qualified. You should participate in this process with your lawyer and make sure that he carefully checks the expert's credentials.

A supreme court judge in a large western city appointed one of her "regular" child psychiatrists, Dr. Smith, to perform a custody evaluation of the Baker family. Dr. Smith was faced with a problem: after a court order decreeing temporary joint custody, Mr. Baker had moved more than two thousand miles away from his spouse, taking his four-year-old daughter with him. As it turned out, Mr. Baker eventually returned to Dr. Smith's city and the psychiatrist was able to interview him there. But Dr. Smith's evaluation of the little girl consisted of, believe it or not, two or three five-minute telephone conversations. He did not have the opportunity of playing with the child or observing her facial expressions. He could not assess her anxiety level. He did not have the opportunity to develop a comfortable relationship with her. Worse, his report was accepted by the court as a complete and legitimate evaluation. The moral is to be healthily skeptical of court-appointed experts and to insist that your lawyer check their credentials and experience.

Despite this caveat, it is still the court-appointed expert who has the most credibility, because he or she is not identified with either side in the dispute. Sometimes a lawyer will want to enlist an expert witness for one side alone. You should discourage this move—for several good reasons—if your lawyer proposed it. First, such a witness, paid by you from the start, will never have the same credibility with the judge that the court-appointed expert commands. In a troubling number of cases, these "hired guns" simply say what the retaining lawyer wants —if the price is right—rather than giving an impartial opinion. (Judges are, however, becoming increasingly aware of this problem and are beginning to downplay the value of such testimony.)

Second, if a court-appointed expert has already been retained to perform an evaluation, involving your child in another round of interviews, it may create more anxiety than it is worth. Third, the evaluation and eventual testimony of such a witness will be limited if he or she has interviewed only those on your side of the case. The expert might assert, for example, that you and your child have an outstanding relationship and that you are a wonderful parent. Yet unless all important parties on the other side have been interviewed as well, the expert will not be able to offer an opinion as to *custody*.

Although your lawyer is bound by professional ethics to do

everything possible within the law to win your case, keep in mind that more does not necessarily mean better when it comes to expert witnesses. If at all possible, try to agree on a qualified, court-appointed expert, and stick with that person.

Let's assume that the judge decides to appoint an expert for your case and the lawyers, pending their respective investigations, agree. What is important now is that you ask your lawyer to screen the potential evaluator. This can usually be done over the telephone. After Dr. Gleason was appointed by the supreme court in New York City to evaluate the Brady family custody dispute, he was contacted by the litigants' lawyers. Mr. Brady's lawyer asked about Dr. Gleason's fee and wanted to know when he could begin the evaluation. But Mrs. Brady's lawyer really grilled the doctor: she not only asked for his résumé, but also inquired about his practice and whether he did anything other than perform custody evaluations. This lawyer was serving her client well, for she knew enough to watch out for the "professional witness"—the practitioner who makes a living by evaluating and testifying in various medical-legal cases. Unfortunately, such professionals may not always be competent or ethical. Mrs. Brady's lawyer was pleased to establish that while Dr. Gleason did conduct custody evaluations with some regularity, and had experience in offering courtroom testimony, he was not a "professional witness."

The lawyer also wanted to know about Dr. Gleason's training in psychiatry, specifically in performing custody evaluations, and she asked if Dr. Gleason was board certified in psychiatry and child psychiatry. (A board-certified psychiatrist has completed postgraduate medical training in psychiatry at an accredited institution and has passed national oral and written examinations administered by a board of prominent physicians. Only about half of this country's psychiatrists are board certified.) She also inquired about the therapist's institutional affiliations and whether he had worked with an experienced custody evaluator or had learned the work on his own. Did Dr. Gleason have a particular philosophy about child custody?

This lawyer was taking the time to look out for her client's best interests by investigating the potential expert's open-mindedness, fairness, and experience. Your lawyer should do no less. He should seek out a board-certified expert—if possible, a doctor affiliated with teaching and clinical institutions: these credentials are impressive. And of course, along with all these professional qualifications, you should not forget to look for equally essential qualities, such as empathy, sensitivity, and the ability to relate comfortably to children.

HOW IS THE expert paid? The generally accepted procedure is for the projected fee to be paid prior to the start of the evaluation. Sometimes, in the heat of the dispute, therapists may not be fully paid for their work by a parent who is angry at the opinion rendered. Because experts need to be protected from such situations, parents should not be offended when they request payment "up front." The usual fee for an evaluation is from two thousand to five thousand dollars, exclusive of court time, which may cost several thousand dollars more. Many experts also require advance payment before they will testify— usually from the party that has requested the court appearance, although the cost will be shared when both parties have an equal interest. In the event of a dispute, the judge will determine who is to pay for the expert's time in court. If you do not think that you can afford the expert's court time, discuss this before the evaluation begins. Perhaps the fee can be adjusted.

☐ CHALLENGING THE EXPERT'S ☐ OPINION

Another way in which an expert witness might become involved in your custody dispute is as a sort of peer reviewer of another expert's evaluation of your case. Let's say that your case is being evaluated by an impartial, court-appointed child psychiatrist. After all the interviews, this expert endorses the contentions of the other side and advises the court that you should not have custody. You and your lawyer believe this expert did not do such an "expert" job, and in fact may have performed a substandard evaluation and submitted a substandard report to the court. What can you do at this point? You can request that another qualified expert review the custody report and comment upon its possible deficiencies.

Dr. Joseph, a child psychiatrist in Virginia, had performed a court-ordered child custody evaluation in the Walters case. He had interviewed all the parties several times and had conducted home visits in order to see the child informally with each parent. At the end of the process, Dr. Joseph wrote a report favoring custody for the child's father. Mrs. Walters and her lawyer were concerned that this report was inadequate and that it was particularly unfair to her. The lawyer asked Dr. Rivera, another child psychiatrist, to review Dr. Joseph's report, and the judge allowed the report to be released to Dr. Rivera.

In her review, Dr. Rivera pointed out that nowhere in Dr. Joseph's report was there any indication as to *why* the father should have custody. She noted that although the report contained little description of the parenting abilities of either parent or of the relationship between each parent and the child, Dr. Joseph had recommended that the father have sole custody. In addition, Dr. Joseph's report included many references to the charges and countercharges made by both sides—hardly the kind of substantive information that can help a judge come to a decision.

Clearly, Dr. Joseph had allowed himself to become involved in the couple's hostilities, had decided that Mrs. Walters was lying while Mr. Walters was telling the truth, and had failed to do his job: to describe either parent's ability to care for the child. Dr. Rivera presented these points in her critique of the original report, and Mrs. Walters' lawyer submitted it to the judge. Impressed by the reviewer's comments, the judge ordered a new custody evaluation by a different child psychiatrist.

Dr. Rivera had been able to steer clear of becoming involved in the custody case itself. As a result, she was able to help the judge see that the custody report was seriously deficient and thus could not be a proper foundation for a decision.

Another case that involved a peer reviewer was the one described earlier involving Dr. Smith, whose evaluation of the Bakers' four-year-old child in their interstate custody dispute was based on several short telephone conversations with her. Dr. Smith had not spent even one full session observing mother and child together, and his report, like Dr. Joseph's, had failed to describe either parent's relationship with their daughter. Without having assessed each parent's fitness or having reviewed the history of their relationships with the child, Dr. Smith nevertheless recommended that the father have sole custody. At this point, the mother and her lawyer retained another child psychiatrist, who, after reviewing Dr. Smith's report, pointed out its deficiencies and agreed to testify on the mother's behalf.

This expert did not offer an opinion as to custody; she could not, because she had not conducted an evaluation herself, and her testimony was therefore limited to a critique of Dr. Smith's report. She explained to the court why the report was inadequate and what questions about the family remained unanswered. Under direct examination by the mother's lawyer, she pointed out that there were certain standards—agreed upon by nationally recognized experts—for performing child custody evaluations, and showed how Dr. Smith had deviated from them. The judge acknowledged her own lack of familiarity with these standards, and was quite interested in this testimony. She questioned the reviewing psychiatrist herself, declared the first report deficient and ordered a new evaluation by another impartial expert.

With so few mental health professionals adequately trained to perform proper child custody evaluations, how can you locate qualified experts? Start first in your own community. Contact the nearest district office of the American Psychiatric Association or the American Academy of Child and Adolescent Psychiatry, both based in Washington, D.C., or the Baltimore-based American Academy of Psychiatry and the Law (see Appendix). This latter organization is made up of psychiatrists who have particular expertise in the area where psychiatry and the law interact. A number of its members perform child custody evaluations.

Have your lawyer inquire at the court whether the judges consult a list of expert witnesses who perform these evaluations. In New York City, for example, custody cases are heard in supreme court and family court, and judges there have a list of child psychiatrists who have demonstrated advanced knowledge and training in such work.

□ THE EVALUATION: □
AN OPPORTUNITY

Assuming that a court-appointed expert has conducted a thorough evaluation, what happens next? The expert will probably have formed an opinion about the best custodial arrangement. In general, that opinion will be expressed in a written report the expert sends to the judge and—depending upon the court's procedures—to both lawyers. Sometimes the expert will request a joint meeting with you and the other parent to present the findings to you both. Some experts make it a practice to hold these meetings after every evaluation—even if one parent does not wish to attend. You may not feel comfortable with this arrangement and you should discuss it with the expert before the start of the evaluation. If you can cope with the possible frustration and anxiety of being in a room together with the other parent, such a meeting might turn out to be beneficial to you both. The expert will share some thoughts with you; possibly he may try to work out some kind of settlement in the hope of preventing a full-blown court battle. Even if you decide to go ahead with the custody suit, you can gain important insights into yourself and your child from such a meeting. So if it is offered to you, don't dismiss it out of hand, particularly if you haven't already been through some other form of mediation. Settling your dispute at this point would be the best possible step you could take on behalf of your child.

Such meetings often distill, for better or worse, the family dynamics that have been at work during the proceedings. After a custody evaluation, Sam and Aurora Martin agreed to meet with Dr. Judith Clarke, the court-appointed expert, to go over her findings and to hear her opinion about custody of their seven-year-old son, Paul. When Dr. Clarke first proposed the meeting to each parent over the phone, Mrs. Martin agreed to attend, but only with great reluctance, while Mr. Martin agreed eagerly and said he hoped it could be a beneficial session for everyone. At the joint session, Dr. Clarke expressed her opinion that Mr. Martin should have custody of Paul, but that Mrs. Martin should be granted extremely liberal visitation privileges.

Mrs. Martin became so angry that she lost control. She lashed out in a fury at both the therapist and her husband. Not only did the meeting fail to resolve the couple's dispute, but Mrs. Martin threatened to engage in years of litigation against her husband for custody of her son. Dr. Clarke's sympathetic counseling about Paul's welfare in the matter was ignored, and the case continued.

On the other hand, after another court-requested custody evaluation, Dr. Clarke met with Syd and Anna Lee. She told them that she thought they would both make adequate parents of Katie, their three-year-old daughter, and offered to help them work out an equitable joint custody arrangement. She also volunteered to make herself available to monitor the arrangement over time. When the Lees agreed, Dr. Clarke met with both parents and their lawyers and helped them work out an arrangement that satisfied everyone. At that point, they were able to end their litigation, each feeling that he or she had "won."

□ THE EXPERT'S REPORT □

If the litigation continues after the kind of joint meeting just described, the expert will send the report of the evaluation to the judge and, if the judge approves, to both lawyers. A responsible therapist will have thought long and hard about what to include in such a report. Even when the choices seem clear, most practitioners cannot help but feel awed by the enormous responsibility entrusted to them, and by the profound impact their recommendation will probably have on this family.

If prepared correctly, the report, usually in the form of a letter directly to the judge, contains the following: a brief introduction stating what questions it will address; a review of who was interviewed, when, and for how long; a list of additional sources, such as other reports the expert might have read; summaries of the clinical interviews the expert conducted along with a general assessment of the individuals seen; and, finally, conclusions and recommendations. The following excerpt, taken from an actual report, will give you an idea of how an expert describes an interview with one parent in a custody dispute:

> During Mr. Blake's private sessions with me, he stressed his own concern about Paula's [his daughter's] welfare and how he believed she was placed in the middle of the marital conflicts. . . . He denied that he is verbally abusive to his daughter, or that he wantonly harasses her. He said that Paula's mother "has a lock on her" and has "brainwashed" her into seeing her father as the enemy. . . . He said that Paula has "a very good mind," but that she is "terribly disoriented" by her mother. Mr. Blake said that he felt certain that he and Paula could have an excellent relationship if only her mother would not interfere. He said that if he received custody of his

daughter, he and she could then work on improving their relationship. . . .

The expert goes on to make specific observations about Mr. Blake:

> During the interview, Mr. Blake presented himself as a highly intelligent and articulate individual with a great deal of expressed anger toward his wife and frustration with his daughter's behavior toward him. . . . He spoke tenderly about his desire to develop a warm relationship with his daughter. . . . He impressed me as genuinely loving Paula and sincerely concerned with her welfare. . . .

Part of a custody evaluation report also includes a description of the expert's sessions alone with the child, where the professional's clinical skills allow for in-depth observation of the child. A good description of what happened should allow the judge to see the child's behavior through the eyes of the therapist. Here is part of another report:

> At the start of the session, Janie [five years old] immediately went to the dollhouse. Reaching for the small dolls I had placed there, she played with them in such a way that they were either repeatedly falling down on the floor, being pushed out the windows, or tripping and falling down the stairs. She included several Transformer fantasy figures in this play, enlisting them to push the children out of the house. The play was quite frenetic and repetitive, and Janie made screaming sounds for the children as they were pushed out the windows of the dollhouse. She explained that the children were being pushed out of the house "because they don't belong there." This repeating play theme is most likely an expression of

the child's uneasiness and psychological distress as she tries to understand her own place in her real house during this time of conflict.

An important part of the evaluation is the description of the sessions in which the child and each parent play together while being observed by the expert. This is admittedly a somewhat artificial environment, and the expert certainly expects parents to be on their best behavior. However, in spite of these limitations, which any good expert would factor into the evaluation, much can be learned from this kind of observed play. Here, from another report, is a description of such a session:

> Linda [four years old] began to play with the puppets while her mother sat at the opposite end of the play table. For most of the session, there was no *interactive* play between them. That is, Linda brought the puppets to the table and played with them for a while, but she did not involve her mother in this play. Likewise, Mrs. Sheldon did not initiate any play with her daughter. Occasionally she would say—almost mechanically—"That's nice, dear," or "Very good, Linda." There was no other spontaneous conversation between them. At one point, toward the end of the session, Linda sneezed four times in a row and then, twice, coughed a deep, raspy cough. Her mother did not respond to this in any way. . . . In general, Mrs. Sheldon appeared uncomfortable at her end of the play table and did not move from her seat during the entire (forty-five minute) session, even though Linda moved around quite a bit.

A rather different picture emerged when this same child was later observed in a play session with her father:

> When Linda started to sneeze and cough, her father immediately responded by getting a tissue and asking

her if she had anything to spit up. Linda said no, but
Mr. Sheldon expressed his concern to me about his
daughter's health. . . . With his daughter at the dollhouse, Mr. Sheldon came over to be near her and sat
on the floor. . . . Later, the two of them worked on
a Lego project together, talking about what they
were building and occasionally chuckling whenever
they had trouble connecting certain pieces together.

How should parents act during these sessions with the child?
Parents should be themselves and behave as they usually do
with their child. The evaluator is interested in give-and-take
between parent and child—not how many times mother hugs
daughter or calls her "Honey." The expert knows parents will
be anxious during these sessions and will think their parenting
skill is being graded. The expert is not looking for a perfect
parent and a good clinician can tell when parental behavior is
forced.

In the final part of the written report, the expert offers the
all-important conclusions and recommendations. This part of
the report should be direct, forthright, practical, realistic, and
free of psychiatric jargon. It should speak directly to the questions at hand and provide real guidance to the judge. Here is an
excerpt from the final section of one such report:

Joint custody is out of the question in this case. Mr.
Franklin is against it, the couple are far apart on many
issues, and they have not demonstrated the slightest
bit of evidence of any commitment to make this form
of custody work. Therefore, the issue here is one of
sole custody. Mrs. Franklin, Beth's mother, should
be granted custody. She has demonstrated her superb
parenting skills, and unlike Beth's father, is far more
acutely aware of this child's special needs and sensi-
tivities. She relates to Beth with a great deal of
warmth and pleasure even in the midst of this tem-
pestuous divorce proceeding. Although Mr. Franklin

> clearly loves his daughter and is concerned about her, his demonstrated level of concern simply does not approach that of the mother. However, he should receive liberal visitation rights . . .

There are two possible outcomes after the judge and the lawyers have reviewed the written report. In one scenario, the report is so convincing that the judge and the lawyers—and both parents—will agree to abide by its recommendations and abandon litigation. This is a therapist's hope, for it means that both sides have recognized the needs of the child and decided to cease hostilities.

The other possibility is that in spite of the findings, the litigation will proceed. Now the expert will probably be called upon to testify in court for the side with which he or she is in agreement.

If, in your case, the therapist believes that you should have custody, you will, of course, feel relieved. If custody goes to the other parent, you will naturally feel disappointed and even angry. However, do not confuse the expert witness with the judge; only the judge makes the decision. The expert offers an opinion—albeit an important one. If she agrees with you, your lawyer will meet with her before the hearing in order to go over her testimony for the all-important court appearance. A therapist with some courtroom experience can often be of great help to a lawyer by advising him on the questions that will elicit important information. The lawyer, for his part, has to prepare the expert for the often anxiety-provoking experience of cross-examination, when she will have to defend the position expressed in the written report. If the expert agrees with the other side, your lawyer will have every opportunity to challenge her testimony in cross-examination, to find fault with the evaluation, and to dissuade the judge from putting much stock in the report.

Whatever the outcome of the trial, the expert might be available afterward to monitor how the decision is carried out and to reassess the needs of the child as they change over time. All of this demonstrates that the expert witness has a crucial role to play in your custody dispute. It is therefore essential that you and your lawyer take care to use the best person you can find. Remember, a judge's recommendation of an expert does not mean that you really *have* an expert. That may indeed be so, but you cannot take it for granted. The resolution of your entire case may rest with the evaluation report. Make sure that it is prepared by a competent, qualified professional.

SOME SPECIAL
ISSUES

CHILD CUSTODY DISPUTES today are complex af-
fairs, but your case may be further complicated by one of many
special circumstances. In this chapter we will look at several
issues that are bringing about changes in custom and law: male
parenting; homosexual parents; allegations of sexual abuse; parental kidnapping; and mental illness.

□ FATHER CUSTODY □

Although the "best interests" presumption is supposed to govern judicial decisions in child custody disputes, many judges still hold to the "tender years" idea, with its preference for the mother. In 1987, for example, a Tennessee state law specified that parental gender should not be considered an issue in a custody case unless the child is of the "tender years"; then it may be a legitimate factor after an examination of parental fitness. In spite of this bias, more and more fathers are seeking custody of their children and challenging the belief that, in general, mothers make better parents.

For too long, fathers as parents were ignored by social scientists and child development researchers. Only in the last twenty-five years has it become apparent that fathers play a profound role in their children's development and that they can provide excellent parenting for girls as well as boys.[1]

Although some researchers have estimated that almost 90 percent of custody awards are made to the mother, single fathers are parenting between one and three million children in this country. Demographic data suggest that single fathers tend to be at higher socioeconomic levels, have higher than average education and income and rate higher in social and economic stability. As a group, single fathers have been found to be caring and nurturing. They often completely change their work and leisure patterns to accommodate their children's needs, are quick to make use of community support and will seek professional advice when necessary. One father left his job to open a home-based business in order to spend time with his young child. Another, a partner in a major law firm, was able to rearrange his busy schedule to pick his children up from school and be home with them most evenings.

Fathers, like mothers, are perfectly capable of forming intense, mutually satisfying, affectional bonds with their children.[2] Studies of fathers as primary parents have generally found their children—even very young infants—to be thriving, vigorous, and psychologically healthy. There is also no evidence to suggest that having a father as the primary caregiver is in any way harmful to the child. Nevertheless, courts will closely examine any father who is seeking sole custody of his children; the examination will take into account his motivation, his ability to parent and to provide for a child's needs, and the age and sex of the child or children.

Should a father have sole custody of a daughter? Some studies suggest that children living with an opposite-sex single parent may have more psychological problems than those who live with a parent of the same sex. However, other studies dispute those conclusions. As more and more courts are beginning to recognize, there is no reason why a father should be denied custody simply because he is a male. The task for the judge—and any expert witness as well—is to assess how well the father in question can meet the specific needs of the child involved. What is the nature of the father-child relationship? Has the father demonstrated that he knows, understands and respects his child? Can he provide for the child's future? In essence, these are the same questions that would be asked of the mother, or of any adult seeking custody of a child. As more fathers seek custody, the courts will become more sensitive to the prejudice against them that now so often prevails in custody cases. For in fact, the paramount concern must always be the best interests of the child.

□   **HOMOSEXUAL PARENTS**   □

When one parent is homosexual, disputes over custody or visitation can be greatly intensified. Now that homosexuality is becoming socially more acceptable, old stereotypes are gradually being challenged. For many adults, being homosexual does not preclude having children or being nurturing and loving parents. Nor does sexual preference imply a life of promiscuity and debauchery. And there is absolutely no evidence that homosexual parents pose any special danger to the health and safety of their children, that they tend to abuse or molest them, or that they attempt to impose their sexual identity upon them.[3]

A growing body of literature in both the social and behavioral sciences attests to the intense research interest in the area of homosexual parenting, and supports the idea that being homosexual and a parent are certainly not mutually exclusive states. National organizations such as the Gay Fathers' Forum and the Lesbian Mothers' National Defense Fund provide support and guidance to gay parents who choose to be actively involved with the growth and development of their children.

Research on gay fathers' parenting shows that they have positive relationships with their sons and daughters as often as fathers who are heterosexual. In fact, according to the experience of clinicians who see homosexual fathers, gay men may try harder than heterosexuals to create stable home lives for their children when they are the sole custodial parent. They tend to be sensitive and nurturing, and often have stable relationships of their own.

Similarly, studies of lesbian mothers suggest that they are no different from heterosexual mothers. They often seek out male figures as role models for their children, and many make a special effort to maintain relationships with former husbands and to involve them in their children's lives. There is no inherent psychopathology in the children of lesbian mothers; these children do not become homosexual at a rate greater than the rest of the population. Girls may tend to worry more than boys about becoming gay if they have a lesbian mother; boys tend to distance themselves more easily from their mothers' sexual orientation. Sons of lesbian mothers tend to rate themselves higher than other boys on scales measuring female-valued traits: gentleness and awareness of another's feelings. Daughters of lesbians, on the other hand, score higher on scales measuring leadership and adventuresomeness, but they are otherwise no different from daughters of heterosexual mothers.

There are very few data on sons of gay fathers, but no evidence to suggest that they are at any greater risk for psychological harm or homosexuality than sons of heterosexual fathers.

They may be disapproving and even ashamed of their father's homosexuality and may require counseling not because their father is gay, but rather to get help in dealing with cultural disapproval of his life-style. Many children of gay fathers can separate their discomfort with the gay identity from their love of their father.

In fact, the biggest problem for children of gay parents seems to be coming to terms with a hostile, uninformed, and judgmental society. They may be ashamed of their mother or father or hurt by the teasing of other children or other parents, but these children are generally able to resolve their feelings about their gay parents with or even without professional counseling.

The growing importance of homosexual parenting as an issue has been reflected in a number of recent court cases and new state laws. In 1987, a San Diego, California, judge awarded custody of a sixteen-year-old boy to his late father's homosexual lover. The judge ruled that the father's lover would give the boy the "stable and wholesome environment" that his mother could not provide. The mother was found to have denied the child visitation with his father when the man was still alive. She had also taken the child illegally and had hidden him for one and a half years. The local probation department found that his mother had "willfully deprived" the youth of his education. The boy's preference was to live with his father's former lover and not with his mother.[4] That same year, on New York's Long Island, a homosexual father was awarded custody of his thirteen-year-old son. The state supreme court judge ruled: "The court finds no evidence of any present or potential harm upon which to make the father's homosexuality a consideration in this custody dispute."[5] Similar findings have also been reached in courts in New Jersey, Massachusetts, and Alaska.

Also in 1987, the South Carolina Court of Appeals and the New York State Supreme Court both held that a parent's homosexuality alone does not in and of itself render that parent unfit to have custody; as always, the standard must be the best interests of the child.[6]

In 1988, the California Court of Appeals reversed a lower court's order prohibiting a father from exercising overnight visitation with his son in the presence of any third person known to be a homosexual. The father, a homosexual himself, shared a town house with two other homosexual men. He was not sexually involved with either of them. The court of appeals ruled that the father's homosexuality did not constitute a danger to the boy and—in the absence of any proof of harm—it was improper to restrict the visitation.[7]

Other state courts, however, have come to very different conclusions, which indicates how much of this particular battle is still to be won! The Virginia Supreme Court found in 1985 that a homosexual man was an "unfit and improper custodian as a matter of law." In 1987, the Missouri Court of Appeals upheld a trial court's decision denying custody to a lesbian mother because of her homosexuality. The court also restricted visitation with this mother because of the presence of her live-in lover. Although the research evidence presented in court failed to show that children were adversely affected by having a homosexual parent, the decision said, in part: "We are not presuming that the wife is an uncaring mother. The environment, however, that she would choose to rear her children in is unhealthy for their growth."[8]

Courts across the United States have been struggling for some time with the issue of homosexuality as it relates to custody disputes, but they are just now beginning to tackle the additional, complicating factor of AIDS. Suits have been filed in Texas, Missouri, Illinois, and New Jersey by heterosexual mothers who maintain that their children are at risk for AIDS when visiting or in the custody of their homosexual father. In a case brought in California, a custodial mother insisted that her homosexual ex-husband have an AIDS test before she would allow their daughters to visit him. In spite of overwhelming evidence that AIDS is not spread by casual contact, this aspect of homosexual parenting and custody disputes is sure to be reflected in court cases for years to come.

• • •

WHAT CAN YOU expect if you are a homosexual parent
involved in a custody battle? Any mental health professional
evaluating a homosexual parent in a child custody or visitation
dispute looks at this adult's activities, home life, parenting
skills, relationship to the child, and the child's feelings and
preferences, just as he does with a heterosexual parent. No
matter what the legal strategy, the psychological issue in this
type of case is not the sexual orientation of the parent, but
which custody or visitation arrangement is in the child's best
interests. A competent, knowledgeable, ethical therapist would
probably agree with the New York and California courts which
have held that being homosexual does not by definition make a
person an unfit parent. And if you are a gay parent—whether
married or divorced—you know that you can be as nurturing
and supportive as any heterosexual adult. However, you may
still be at a distinct disadvantage in a custody dispute if your
homosexuality is known.

For one thing, you should expect an unpleasant courtroom
experience. The lawyer for the other side may question you
with hostility, sarcasm, or mock ignorance about homosexuality to try to discredit you. You may be asked absurd and insulting questions, such as whether you have ever been charged
with molesting little girls or boys, whether you parade around
in clothing belonging to the opposite sex, and when and what
your own first sexual experience was. Many of these questions
will be met by objections from your lawyer, and you will
probably not have to answer them. However, they are designed
to intimidate, frighten, and unnerve you. The more you anticipate these kinds of questions, the better you will be able to
deal with them in a reasonably calm manner. '

Your best preparation, then, will be to show why you are as
good a parent as you say you are and why your homosexuality
is irrelevant to the quality of your parenting. Make sure your
lawyer gives you time to testify about the history of your parenting. You could relate your involvement with your child

from infancy onward, your attention to her emotional and physical needs, your sensitivity to her unique characteristics, your being there for everything from bandaging a skinned knee to driving the child to a friend's home, your involvement in school, your role in religious training, if any, and so on. This is what the judge will want to know, and these are the true issues she should be considering. Judges, however, are as vulnerable to prejudice as other people; your job will be to try and make a case that provides enough information to challenge such a prejudice. And your best strategy is to reveal or downplay your homosexuality as you would in any situation. If it is not an issue, you shouldn't make it one.

If, on the other hand, it is the other parent in the dispute who is homosexual, you may be angry and frightened, and you and your lawyer may decide to make this an important issue in the case. But making your spouse's homosexuality an issue is valid only if you can show that the homosexuality is part of other behaviors that may be detrimental to your child. In other words, claiming parental homosexuality is not enough to prove inadequate parenting. Does the homosexual parent force the child to favor homosexuality as a life-style? That is, is the child proselytized? Is the child in any danger with this parent? Bear in mind that a stereotype that makes a homosexual parent synonymous with a child molester is without foundation and as unfair as any other kind of prejudice. If you cannot go beyond saying that the other parent is homosexual, it is not a legitimate argument. Whatever the particular circumstance, you need to understand all aspects of this emotion-laden issue so that you can make informed decisions on behalf of your child.

□ ALLEGATIONS OF □
SEXUAL ABUSE

In the past decade, our society has become increasingly aware of childhood sexual abuse and incest. These problems, well known to mental health professionals, are now increasingly encountered by lawyers, law enforcement officials, and judges. Along with heightened public awareness has come an increase in the number of divorcing wives accusing their husbands of sexually abusing the children. These allegations often surface during the course of custody and visitation disputes. Once the charge is made, it acts like kerosene poured on the already roaring flames of the litigation. You need to understand the impact such an accusation could have on you and your children.

A supreme court judge in an eastern state asked a child psychiatrist to evaluate the Lamays. In the midst of their divorce action, and after months of uncontested living and visitation arrangements, Susan Lamay had brought an action against her husband, Paul, to deny him overnight visitation with his two sons and daughter. She claimed that he was insisting the children take turns sleeping with him at night, and that this activity was detrimental to the children's welfare. The judge had issued a temporary order blocking the overnight visits pending the outcome of the psychiatric evaluation.

During the evaluation, Susan Lamay did not directly accuse her husband of physically or sexually harming the children, although she did express the fear that this would or could happen at any time. She said it was improper for an eleven-year-old daughter or six- and seven-year old sons to sleep with their father, especially if they were being forced to do so. Paul Lamay, while acknowledging that the children had slept with him from time to time, denied that he had forced them or that he was abusing them in any way. In fact, he maintained that one son initially slept with him because his wife, after moving out of the marital bed (but not the home), had taken that son's room. Subsequently, Paul said, the other children, feeling deprived of contact with their father, began to take turns sleeping with him. He contended that Susan was fully aware of this arrangement but that she had not protested it until the lawyers for both sides had become deadlocked over the financial settlement.

The psychiatric evaluation revealed no evidence of abuse or sexual molestation. The children were devoted to their father and were distraught that their mother was making an issue of what they said they did only once in a while. They denied that their father touched them sexually, and all appeared quite comfortable in the session with him. Mr. Lamay admitted to the psychiatrist that he had probably used poor judgment in agreeing to this sleeping arrangement. However, he insisted that he had meant no harm, that in the Philippines, where he had grown up, this arrangement was quite common, and that in any case he would not allow it to continue. The psychiatrist believed that the mother in this case had made a mountain out of a molehill, and urged the judge to restore overnight visitation. This was immediately done.

Allegations of sexual abuse may be difficult to substantiate. When they occur during the turmoil of a custody dispute, they may be even harder to evaluate. Certain characteristics of some actual cases, however, may help the evaluating expert to ascertain what really happened. In a substantiated case, the initial charges often come from the child—after some delay and with some reticence—and not from the parent. The child may become depressed and anxious, and drawings and play may be consonant with the allegation of sexual abuse—that is, children may draw something that represents what happened to them, or their play may reflect the emotional trauma they suffered. A doll might have a secret or be sad because someone has hurt her, or the child may tell a story about the doll being in danger. An abused child may show extreme anxiety in the abuser's presence and refuse to repeat an account of the experience. In addition, the child's use of language when describing the experience is often consistent from one time to another.

In cases that turn out to be false, the child may disclose the "information" all too readily and with little evidence of anxiety or depression. The child's language may reflect prompting by an adult, and the child may not seem distressed when with the "abuser." The qualifier "may" has been used often in this context because, in fact, there is no sure way—short of uncovering definite physical evidence—to differentiate between true and false allegations of sexual abuse.

Why do some parents knowingly make false accusations of sexual abuse during custody battles? They may be angry and vindictive and wish to take some kind of revenge upon the other. They may be so angry, in fact, that they fail to see how they are using their children in a very unhealthy way. A mother making a false allegation may wish to rid herself of a man she sees as a poor husband and bad father and bring the litigation to a halt. (Most allegations, true or false, originate with the mother.) She may be dissatisfied with the custody or visitation arrangement that exists or is being negotiated, and may feel that the allegation will influence the judge. Or she may herself be suffering from a psychiatric disorder that distorts her perceptions of reality. Signs of paranoia or a severe personality disorder may be subtle enough to be missed by the judge, the lawyers, and sometimes even the psychiatrist.

There is no doubt among mental health professionals that more and more cases of actual, unequivocal sexual abuse of children (in and out of custody disputes) are being reported. Yet practitioners disagree about how widespread a problem false allegations are. It is clear that false charges—primarily against fathers—do occur, especially during custody litigation. Unfortunately, even the most experienced child psychiatrists and psychologists cannot always tell the difference. Children react in a variety of ways to abuse and molestation as well as to prompting by a parent. There is no specific sex abuse syndrome that can provide the answer.

If you are firmly convinced or highly suspicious that the other parent is indeed causing harm to your child, then of course you are obligated to protect her. However, if you (or your lawyer) are thinking of using this issue as a legal tactic, or to punish the other parent, don't! Think hard before you add to your child's distress and subject her to what could be simply another form of abuse.

Once an allegation of sexual abuse is made, the child may be exposed to countless interviews. She may have to speak to doctors, social workers, the police, your lawyer, your pediatrician, and a psychiatrist, as well as to the district attorney and the judge. Some places have better systems for evaluating such allegations than others. But sometimes, even with the best system, a small child may be evaluated numerous times. (If the child is fortunate, the district attorney, the police, and the court will have worked out an arrangement so that only one person does the interviews.)

During these meetings, the interviewer first tries to establish a comfortable and trusting relationship with the child. This may or may not happen readily. The interviewer will then try to elicit from the child whether or not there has been any abuse, and if so, of what kind, as well as who committed it. The interviewer may do this directly, by asking the child, or indirectly, by observing the child at play, body language, drawings, and so on. Sometimes the interviewer may use "anatomically correct" dolls. The child may be asked the names of various body parts, their function, and whether anyone has touched her or him on those parts.

Different interviewers work differently. There is no one correct way to interview a child after allegations of sexual abuse. What most people agree on, however, is that these interviews are stressful for parents as well as for children. And they are, unfortunately, often conducted by inexperienced people.

So before you allege sexual abuse during your custody battle, be sure you have real grounds. And be sure that whoever is investigating the allegation is a well-trained professional, someone specially prepared to evaluate sexual abuse. Sometimes the investigation can be done by the same expert witness who is evaluating your custody dispute. But keep in mind that not all psychiatrists and psychologists who evaluate custody disputes are also trained to evaluate allegations of sexual abuse. Investigate these people carefully, just as you do any other expert involved with your child. Do everything you can to protect your child from further emotional trauma.

If you are accused of sexually abusing your child and you are innocent and know the allegation is frivolous, plan a calm and rational strategy. Do not involve the child at all! Do not put him in the witness box in order to clear your name. Do not talk with the media! Even though you may be overwhelmed by feelings of anger and a sense of outrage, do not let yourself be swept away by the feelings of the moment. Tell your child that this is something you and the other parent will have to work out, and that the judge will help too. You will be sparing your child further pain.

Of course, our emphasis on the danger of making false charges of sexual abuse certainly should not lead you to ignore or deny sexual abuse that is real. But because you might be tempted or advised to exaggerate the sins of the other side in the service of some legal strategy, it is important for you to realize how much harm this kind of charge can do.

□ PARENTAL KIDNAPPING □

During the course of a child custody dispute, probably every parent has at one time or another had the fantasy of running off with the child and starting a new life elsewhere. Most don't, of course. They realize that this would complicate things even more, that it might be psychologically harmful to the child, and that it also could result in severe legal repercussions. Parents could be jailed, or they might lose custody of the child, or their visitation rights might be severely limited. Nevertheless, although precise figures are difficult to gather, tens of thousands of parental kidnappings take place each year.[9] Many of these kidnapped children are never found.

Parents who kidnap do so out of a variety of motives: they may fear losing the case or the child, they may be unhappy with the custody or visitation arrangement decided by the court, or may be motivated by a variety of other strong impulses. In some instances, the abducting parent can suffer from a psychological problem. For example, a mother may have great difficulty separating her own private needs from those of her child. She may blame the father for all her problems and see him as totally evil; if she does, then she has a rationale—unrealistic as it might be—for keeping her child away from this "bad" parent. The same dynamic can apply to a father.

In fact, more fathers than mothers kidnap their children. Their motives may range from wanting revenge on the other parent for perceived past injustices, to fear of losing the case, to the conviction that they are the better parent. There are no data to explain this phenomenon, but possible causes range from the fact that there are still fewer fathers granted sole custody than mothers, to the observation that men may simply have more opportunity than women, given their "advantages" in terms of money, mobility, and independence.

Many cases of parental kidnapping are discovered only when one parent goes to the home of the other to pick up the child and finds no one there. This happened in the Robbins family, when Bart Robbins took four-year-old Terence away just hours before his mother was due to arrive. Mr. Robbins told his son that his mother did not want to see him any more and was not interested in him. He said that he and Terence were going to a new home to find "a new mommy." Mr. Robbins had planned everything very carefully and had covered his trail well. In fact, it took Terence's mother—with the help of private detectives and a sympathetic relative of Mr. Robbins— three years to locate her son.

Mr. Robbins took Terence to a state halfway across the country from his mother. Some parents take their children to other countries. The Department of State has estimated that every year between three hundred and four hundred children are kidnapped by a parent and taken out of the United States to live. Thanks to a new federal law passed in 1988, parents of abducted children will no longer face great obstacles in recovering children taken to other countries. The new law enables the U.S. government to implement a treaty, already ratified by the Senate, that provides for the prompt return of children abducted to a foreign country and for visitation rights across international boundaries. By 1990, nine other countries will have ratified the treaty: Canada, Great Britain, France, Portugal, Switzerland, Hungary, Luxembourg, Australia, and Spain.

Until recently, parents were exempted from federal and state kidnapping statutes. Nor were courts of one state compelled to honor the custody decrees of other states. The Uniform Child Custody Jurisdiction Act of 1968 (now law in nearly every state in the country) was passed to help identify the state in which a custody case should be heard. This law takes into account where the child has lived in the six months prior to the beginning of legal proceedings, where the custodial parent lives, and how the child's interests would best be served. The Parental Kidnapping Prevention Act of 1980 allows parental kidnapping cases to be investigated by the FBI provided that the act is a felony in the state from which the child was taken.

However, in a setback for those who feel the states' policies are not uniform enough to deal with kidnapping cases, the U.S. Supreme Court ruled in 1988 that federal courts could not be asked to resolve interstate custody disputes. (Child advocacy groups, such as the National Council for Children's Rights, had urged the Supreme Court to allow the federal courts jurisdiction in these cases.) Congress has been asked to resolve the matter with new legislation that will strengthen the Parental Kidnapping Prevention Act by allowing federal courts to intervene in interstate disputes when no other solution is forthcoming.

WHAT EFFECT DOES parental kidnapping have upon children? First, they may become extremely upset by an unauthorized absence with a parent, even if it lasts only hours or days. Jon and Ellen Rudolph, nine-year-old twins, normally visited their father every other weekend and during school vacations. Over one spring break he had wanted to take them to Europe. His ex-wife had refused, saying it was not "convenient." Acting out of frustration, Mr. Rudolph picked up his children for their weekend with him, drove directly to the airport and flew with them to Paris that night. He called his ex-wife after arriving in Paris and told her he would bring the children back in one week.

Jon and Ellen were excited, but they were also confused. They knew that what they were doing was wrong, but they were also thrilled to be with their father in another country. Although they never feared that they would not be brought home, they were still anxious. They could not really relax and enjoy the trip. In fact, Jon vomited several times, and Ellen complained about a headache.

Upon their return, the children were agitated and restless. Jon had trouble sleeping, and Ellen was sent home from school twice during the first week back. Her teacher phoned Mrs. Rudolph to report that Ellen was crying during class for no apparent reason.

More serious abductions can result in extensive psychological trauma for the child. Sometimes a child is kidnapped, retrieved, and kidnapped again. The child, moved rapidly and without notice from one location to another, will often be asked to lie about her identity. Schooling is disrupted. Ties with friends and relatives are severed. Under such conditions, a child may experience long-term difficulty in trusting others, have poor relationships with peers and suffer separation anxiety, fearfulness, and general nervousness. Over a long period of time, the abducted child may come to reject the parent from whom she has been separated. The child, in effect, becomes "brainwashed" by the kidnapping parent, convinced that the other parent did not come to her rescue because she was not loved and wanted. Thus, even if a child is returned to the other parent, she may resent being back and act as if she hates that parent —withholding any form of affection or becoming verbally or physically abusive. Yet this behavior may be confusing and distressing for the child because she still loves that parent. And conversely, the child will have felt similarly mixed emotions toward the kidnapping parent, often seeming unclear about how to behave, or what to say or do. Confusion and anger prevail—kidnapping is but a Pyrrhic victory for the kidnapper.

Kidnapping is indeed a desperate act. It is unsettling, potentially traumatic for the child, and always illegal. The abducting parent, believing he or she is acting in the child's best interests, may very well be increasing the trauma the child has already suffered during the custody or visitation dispute. Kidnapping may seem to be the best solution to a difficult dilemma, but it soon becomes a new problem in its own right, compounding the tragedy of the custody battle for parents and children alike.

□   **THE MENTALLY ILL PARENT**   □

Child psychiatrists who evaluate custody disputes often encounter the allegation that one of the parents has or has had a severe psychiatric illness, such as schizophrenia, manic-depressive disease, depression, severe anxiety, or an addiction. (Being in therapy is not usually taken to be a sign of mental illness, since many people seek professional help during stressful times in their lives.) If a history of mental illness is known, the opposing lawyer will often use it as an argument against that parent's being awarded custody or liberal visitation rights. In such a situation, most judges will request a psychiatric evaluation in order to make an informed decision. The evaluation is usually part of the regular custody investigation of the entire family.

Bonnie Black, a nine-year-old living in Massachusetts with her mother and stepfather, often visited her father, who lived in New York. He had a history of alcoholism. For various reasons, Bonnie's mother felt that Bonnie's visits with her father should be restricted. For one thing, she was convinced that he was still abusing alcohol, and did not want him to drive with his daughter. She also believed that being alone with an alcoholic father—even once or twice a month and for parts of vacations—was detrimental to Bonnie's psychological health. The case was being tried in New York, and a supreme court judge there asked a child psychiatrist to evaluate the family and offer an opinion about the relationship between father and daughter.

The evaluation of Jerome Black revealed a man clearly devoted to his daughter. He had always participated in her care.

In the three years since the divorce, he had consistently provided child support payments and had maintained a regular visitation routine. He had never failed to arrive after saying he would visit, and he insisted that he and Bonnie had always had an excellent relationship. Mr. Black denied that he was an alcoholic. He said he did enjoy drinking and from time to time probably drank too much. He reported having about three beers and two to three glasses of wine at night, along with an occasional Scotch before going to bed. He said he did not abuse alcohol when he was with Bonnie and had never driven anywhere with her while impaired by it.

Mr. Black did, however, admit to pleading guilty to driving while intoxicated two years before. He said that he had been alone at the time, on his way home from a New Year's Eve party. The psychiatrist noted during the evaluation that Mr. Black had a fine tremor of the hands and lips and red lesions on the skin of his hands and face—all signs suggestive of chronic alcoholism.

Alone with the psychiatrist, Bonnie told him that she loved her father very much and wished to continue her regular visits with him. She said that they had an easy, warm relationship, that they went places together as well as just "hanging out." Because he was an artist, her father could help her with her art work, and she said he was extremely supportive; neither her mother nor her new stepfather knew much about art. However, Bonnie also mentioned that she knew her father abused alcohol because she found empty wine bottles near his bed in the mornings. Once, about a year before, she said, he had been drinking beer while driving with her. This had upset her and she had asked him never to do it again. He hadn't. Bonnie had not told her mother about this, because she feared an interruption of the visits with her father.

The joint interview with Mr. Black and his daughter demonstrated their easy, affectionate relationship. There was clearly a strong bond between them. The evaluating psychiatrist observed no evidence of any strain or anxiety in the child. At one point during this session, in fact, Bonnie said spontaneously, "I don't ever want to stop seeing him. He's my real father, and I love him a lot. And you can tell my mother I said that!"

In his report to the judge, the psychiatrist described the warm relationship between father and daughter. He stated that although he believed Jerome Black was alcoholic, this fact did not in and of itself militate against visits with Bonnie. In fact, the doctor went on, to deprive the child of these visits would be extremely detrimental to her welfare. However, the report did suggest that Mr. Black not be allowed to drive Bonnie anywhere; some other mode of transportation would have to be arranged.

The issue here was not the diagnosis of alcoholism itself but rather what effect the illness was having on the parent–child relationship—a question that must be taken into account during any evaluation for custody or visitation. The child psychiatrist, in evaluating a parent who may have a mental illness, wants to know if it is intermittent or chronic and specifically, whether the condition endangers the child in any way. What ameliorating factors are present to offset the illness? For example, are there grandparents, other relatives, or friends who can be supportive? What is the prognosis? Is the parent receiving treatment and complying with a doctor's recommendations? If lithium has been prescribed for a manic-depressive, is it used according to instructions and together with regular visits to a psychiatrist? Does the parent deal with the illness in a realistic way, or is there denial and refusal to deal with the condition? How does the child regard the parent's illness? What has this parent–child relationship been like in the past? These are important questions that go beyond the fact of mental illness to examine a parent's ability to continue caring for a child. The psychiatrist will assess the parent's strengths as well as weaknesses and make recommendations accordingly.

Sometimes the mental illness of a parent does indeed interfere with the relationship to the child and even puts the child in danger. When that happens, the child must be protected, and the decision about custody or visitation must be influenced by the psychiatric condition of the parent. Here is one such case.

Mr. and Mrs. Emory were involved in a custody dispute regarding their daughter Sara, age four. It was acknowledged by the court, by both sides, and by the court-appointed child psychiatrist that five years before, Arthur Emory had been a patient in a psychiatric hospital and had been diagnosed as having schizophrenia, paranoid type. According to hospital records, he had become increasingly suspicious of his neighbors and members of his family, had called the police numerous times to report alleged attempts on his life and had eventually jumped into a nearby river, supposedly to escape people who were plotting against him. After two months, he was discharged from the hospital on antipsychotic medication, but one year prior to the evaluation had decided not to take it any longer. Instead, he went to a "nutritional psychiatrist," who told him that his paranoia was caused by food allergies and prescribed a special diet. Mr. Emory followed this for a few months, but then abandoned it. However, for some time he manifested no outward signs of emotional illness.

At the time of the custody battle, Mr. Emory was seeing his daughter once during the week and every weekend, in accordance with a temporary arrangement decreed by the court. Over the last few months, he had been taking his daughter to hospital emergency rooms on each day of her visit with him, claiming that she was being abused by her mother, had been poisoned by food or milk, had strange marks on her body, or was being given dangerous drugs. During a three-month period, Sara had received fourteen physical examinations. On each of these occasions, the emergency-room doctor failed to find any abnormality. In addition, the city agency that handled child abuse charges had made three separate investigations. All concluded that the charges were unfounded.

During the psychiatric evaluation, Mr. Emory spoke at length about his belief that his ex-wife was poisoning Sara and inflicting small cuts and burns on her arms, legs, and chest. When asked why no doctor had ever substantiated these charges, Mr. Emory replied that the doctors were collaborating with Alice Emory, who was, in turn, rewarding them financially. Although his behavior was not bizarre and he knew the day, date, year, etc., Mr. Emory's conversation was full of references to plots against him, dangerous enemies of his daughter, and doctors, police, and other officials who were "lying" and "covering up."

Alice Emory insisted that her ex-husband's charges were false. She told the psychiatrist she was extremely worried about the emotional toll this confusing situation was taking on Sara. She expressed her fear that the frequent physical examinations her daughter was being made to undergo were in themselves a form of child abuse. And she did not want Sara to be alone with her father.

At the end of the family evaluation, the psychiatrist agreed with Mrs. Emory and warned the court that in this case, Mr. Emory's mental illness, clearly not under control at the time, was extremely detrimental to the child. He stated that in his medical opinion, Mr. Emory suffered from a paranoid condition involving delusions about Sara's being continually harmed. These delusions themselves were in fact harming Sara. Since Mr. Emory refused to acknowledge the fact that he suffered from a mental illness and because he was not interested in receiving any treatment for it, the court could assume that his damaging behavior toward his daughter would probably continue and might even escalate. The psychiatrist recommended that Mrs. Emory receive custody and that Sara's visits with her father be carefully supervised—that a neutral third party (a neighbor or a friend) be present when parent and child were together.

From the two cases documented here, it should be clear that the issue of mental illness must be considered in the context of the particular family. Of paramount importance is how the parents deal with the illness and its effects upon the parent-child relationship. Mental illness is a legitimate issue in litigation if, and only if, it can be shown to be detrimental to the best interests of the child. Otherwise, it is not relevant.

If you have or have had a psychiatric illness and it has become an issue in your custody case, what should you do? Don't panic, don't lie, and don't feel ashamed! Instead, review the history of the illness and the impact it has had on yourself and your child. The judge will be more interested in how you have dealt with the illness than in the fact that you have had a psychiatric disorder. If you require medication, make sure you are able to show that you take it regularly and according to your doctor's orders. Be sure to stress as well that you are taking care of yourself and show the steps you have taken to mitigate the effects of your illness on your relationship with your child. Demonstrate willingness to undergo regular psychotherapy, if that is required. Collect receipts for past therapy bills, or get a letter from your therapist indicating that you have been a regular patient. Rather than expending a great deal of energy minimizing a past or chronic illness, you can go a long way toward making it a nonissue if you can show how well you are able to cope and that having such an illness does not affect your ability to be a loving parent.

□ THE NONBIOLOGICAL □
PARENT

Until the 1980s, custody suits brought by nonbiological parents or parent surrogates were rare—and next to impossible to win. Most judges were reluctant to remove children permanently from their natural parents except in cases of repeated abuse or neglect: so-called termination of parental rights cases. The courts were guided by a long history of judicial preference for natural parents.

In recent years, however, the high divorce rate, coupled with the rising number of families composed of unrelated individuals, has produced more custody and visitation disputes involving natural parents versus nonbiological parents. In the United States, one out of five children now lives in a stepfamily, and a thousand new stepfamilies form every day. They break up too. Albeit with some reluctance, judges have decided in a number of cases to award custody, or major visitation rights, to the nonbiological parent or to another adult instead of to the natural parent. At least a dozen states have passed laws that give stepparents the right to sue for custody or visitation after a divorce. Again, the presumption of judges in these cases is the best interests of the child.[10]

In one such visitation case, Edward Cody was seeking visitation of Justin, age seven. Edward and his ex-wife, Phyllis, had had no children during their two-year marriage. However, eighteen months after the divorce was declared final, Phyllis became pregnant and informed Edward that he was the father. (They had continued to date and to have sexual relations.) Edward did not contest this assertion, and in fact paid his ex-wife's prenatal medical expenses and the hospital bill. He also was present at the delivery of his son, and helped Phyllis care for the child. Edward, Phyllis, and Justin then lived together intermittently until Phyllis moved out permanently, taking Justin with her. Even after this separation, Justin and Edward were together several times a week and during some part of every weekend. When Justin was four years old, Phyllis became involved with another man.

At this point, Phyllis began to cut down on Edward's visitation with Justin. She canceled scheduled visits and used various excuses. After some time had passed, Edward demanded to see his son. It was then that Phyllis informed him that she had lied to him and that, in fact, he was not Justin's real father! Shocked and disbelieving, Edward took a blood test and had Justin take one as well. The tests proved Phyllis correct: Edward was definitely excluded as Justin's biological father.

Nevertheless, Edward hired a lawyer and went to court to force the issue of visitation. At the hearing, the judge learned that Edward and Justin, for all intents and purposes, had a long-standing and mutually satisfying father-son relationship. Evidence was presented proving Edward's history of involvement with the child he had always thought of as his own. Justin, in turn, had been told by his mother that Edward was his father. He called him "Pa." Now, at age seven, the child would have to deal with the news that this man was not his real father.

Edward insisted that his relationship with Justin was extremely important to the child's development, and that it should not be curtailed. The judge agreed. Full visitation rights were restored to Edward.

In this case, the judge was persuaded that the best interests of the child would be served by continued contact with Edward, his psychological if not his biological father. The judge wisely assessed the potential harm to Justin if the relationship were ended. In other cases, judges have acted similarly. For example, the Connecticut Supreme Court ruled in 1984 that in a custody dispute between a child's surviving parent and the grandparents, there is no presumption of fitness on the part of the biological parent. The court said: "The genetic connection is not determinative of the best interests of the child, although it is certainly a factor." This court affirmed an award of custody to a child's grandparents. In 1987, the Michigan Court of Appeals adopted the concept of "equitable parent," which allows a non-biological father to sue for custody or visitation. The criteria for the legitimacy of such a suit in Michigan are that the child was born during a marriage, that the child and father developed a legitimate father-son relationship over time, that the mother encouraged the relationship, that the father provided financial support for the child, that the father remained actively involved with the child even after the separation, and that the child and the man would suffer serious psychological harm if the relationship were to be curtailed or terminated.

Sometimes a stepparent will bring a custody suit against the natural parent when the marriage dissolves. If the judge accepts that the presumption of the best interests of the child can override blood relationships, it is possible for custody to be awarded to the stepparent. The Barris family exemplifies this unusual situation.

Mr. and Mrs. Barris had been married for eight years. It was Mr. Barris's second marriage; he had a daughter, Violet, thirteen, from his previous marriage. The Barrises also had their own natural child, Peter, who was four. One of the major reasons for the breakup of the marriage was the fact that Mr.

Barris suffered from a paranoid psychotic disorder. He constantly accused his wife of infidelity, although there was no basis for his claims, and he interpreted the most innocent things in the environment as signs of plots against him. He believed Mrs. Barris was part of a secret government agency tracing his every move. He refused any psychiatric help, saying that people were trying to poison his mind.

Mr. Barris refused to give his wife custody of the children, and a court battle ensued. His lawyer argued that psychiatrically ill or not, Mr. Barris was Violet's natural father and therefore had the right to be the sole custodial parent. The lawyer for Mrs. Barris argued that she had acted in all respects as Violet's mother for the past eight years and that she had an extremely close relationship with the child. Furthermore, Violet's best interests would be served by having Mrs. Barris as her parent, rather than her biological father, whose psychiatric disorder promised to be chronic. The judge agreed, and Mrs. Barris was awarded sole custody of her stepdaughter, along with custody of Peter.

Most judges would still prefer to award custody to a natural parent over a nonbiological parent or guardian. Yet as this case shows, the courts as a rule do respect the presumption of the best interests of the child, even if the details vary from case to case. In situations like those presented here, judges will often render courageous decisions out of a sincere desire to protect the child.

How judges reach decisions in custody disputes—and what the experience is like for parents going to court—are the subjects of the next two chapters.

YOUR DAY
IN COURT

PERHAPS THE TITLE of this chapter should read "Your Days in Court," for custody cases can drag on and on. Among the agonies of a custody dispute are the long delays and postponements that seem to occur at every turn. Waiting for your case to be heard can be the ultimate test of endurance, as you grit your teeth through the legal maneuvering, depositions, correspondence, charges, and countercharges. And you can't count on an easier time once the trial has actually begun, for delays can occur even during the hearing itself. You should try to anticipate and allow for the inevitable tension that these delays will cause you and your children. You can just about count on something throwing off your timetable, either before or during the trial—or both.

These delays, so common in the adversarial system, can be caused by either the lawyers or the judges. Lawyers postpone or delay trials when they believe certain issues that affect their clients warrant such action. Remember, however, most lawyers are as anxious to reach a resolution as you are and do not enjoy the prolonged litigation. But in order to fulfill the obligation to best represent you, your lawyer may have to seek a postponement while she introduces a new motion, deposes another witness, or waits for the testimony of a particular witness who is available only at certain times. (This may often be the case with medical experts.) And even during your trial, your lawyer might decide that a change in strategy or the introduction of an important new witness is worth a delay.

Sometimes judges are forced to postpone or delay cases as well. In some cities, judges are absolutely inundated with cases. Your trial, certainly of paramount importance to you, is but one of many to even the most caring of judges. Postponements may be caused by the pressures and complexities of the court calendar: other cases may intervene or the judge may be called to preside over an unexpected hearing or to review a new motion in another case. Or, during the trial, a judge might have to put off completion because the court stenographer is ill or has to go home early and has no replacement. Another judge might interrupt the proceedings because of a family crisis or illness. Be philosophical about these delays, or you will be frustrated beyond endurance.

Proponents of litigation argue that court delays allow each side the opportunity to cool off and perhaps come to some agreement. But as we have observed throughout this guide, extended proceedings can be psychologically harmful to children. How can you best prepare yourself and your children for the court experience? This emotional work is as necessary and as significant as all the legal work you and your lawyer have done. And as you prepare yourself and your children for what is to come, remember that others will be taking part as well. This chapter describes how the expert witness, your child, and you can prepare for—and survive—this ordeal.

Let's assume that after months and months of preparation, your lawyer informs you that a court date has been set. If you are fortunate, it will be just a few months away. As the date approaches, you may get quite anxious, imagining all kinds of things. When you are finally sitting in the courtroom, you will appreciate the almost existential absurdity of the situation. Once you embarked upon this custody dispute, you probably felt upon occasion that things were out of your control. You will certainly feel this now. You watch silently as the judge takes a seat and the court reporter settles down before the stenograph machine. Your lawyer shuffles papers. The other lawyer leans over to whisper something to your adversary, someone you once loved and were married to. You stare at the American flag, the floor, the walls, your fingernails. You ask yourself how it all came to this. You think of your children. You wonder if you have made a big mistake. You may even say a prayer. The trial begins. Are you ready?

□   PREPARING THE WITNESS   □

The expert witness, if there is one in your case, may be a source of help in preparing for trial. If the expert's opinion following the evaluation coincides with your position, then your lawyer will have to decide whether or not that expert ought to testify for your side. In some cases, he may feel that the expert's report stands up very well on its own and does not require a court appearance. (If the other side decides to call the expert to testify in an attempt to refute her conclusions, your lawyer will have the opportunity to question her.)

If your lawyer does decide to have the expert testify on your behalf, make sure the two of them meet beforehand to plan the testimony. A quick telephone conversation won't do. The lawyer–expert witness meeting provides an opportunity for each to guide the other through the testimony and to get to know each other's style. The lawyer might let the expert know that he will begin direct examination by establishing the expert's credentials. He might ask for educational background, number of years in training, board certification, hospital affiliations, teaching positions, publications, previous experience in performing custody evaluations, and so on. The expert may be asked how many evaluations she has performed and how many hours were spent on yours. It will be important for her to have this information at hand so that the testimony goes smoothly.

Your lawyer might then let the expert know how he will conduct the rest of the examination, what questions he will ask first, and what the general sequence of questions will be. A good lawyer conducts questioning as if he were constructing a geometric proof. Make sure yours has such a strategy with each witness he plans to call.

The expert, in turn, can help the lawyer with the testimony. She might suggest that the lawyer pursue certain lines of questioning to elicit important information about the children's relationships with you and the other parent. She can help the lawyer ask specific questions about the children's developmental level and temperament which will allow the court to appreciate what they are experiencing. In addition, she can make sure the lawyer's questions are child-oriented and specific enough to help the judge get to know your children. Moreover, the expert can help the lawyer with any potential weaknesses in the testimony, explain why they might be there, and suggest ways of dealing with them. And if the expert neglected to interview someone important in the case, or forgot to ask a relevant question, now is the time to mention this and to plan how to contend with the barrage of hostile questions it is likely to evoke.

The expert and your lawyer should also use this preparation time to anticipate the cross-examination. Assuming that the expert's opinion supports your position, your own lawyer's direct examination will be easy, comfortable, respectful, and friendly. The cross-examination, on the other hand, may be just the opposite. The purpose of the "cross" is to refute the testimony heard during direct examination, to minimize it, to criticize it, and to point out its weaknesses, deficiencies, and misperceptions.

Mental health professionals should expect the usual skeptical questions about the apparently "soft" science of psychiatry: Don't psychiatrists often differ about diagnoses? Isn't it true that in spite of recent advances in neurobiology, no one really understands human behavior or motivation? Isn't it true that psychiatrists can be fooled and may not be able to detect when people are lying? In addition, the opposing lawyer may point out that it is ludicrous to assume that after a few office visits, a child psychiatrist will know enough about a family to recommend which parent should have custody. Finally, the cross-examiner may attempt to discredit the credentials of the expert witness (if she failed to make such an attempt at the start of the expert's direct testimony).

This kind of strategy must always be expected, and your lawyer and the expert can decide how best to handle it. The expert can explain that in the field of psychiatry, despite its apparent "softness," those who have been specially trained now know a great deal about children's emotional lives and their development and growth. This is not necessarily quantifiable information, but it is nonetheless very valuable, as is the experts' experience with the complexity of family dynamics. The expert can also testify that she has been paid for her *time* in court—not her testimony. If she is asked what payments she has received, she should honestly and calmly answer the question without being defensive or arrogant. She can say that the time spent performing the custody evaluation was necessarily limited, and that the office setting was of course an artificial one. However, as an expert in child development, child behavior, and families, she can express confidence that she had enough time to diagnose your situation and to provide important and relevant information to the court.

As we have noted, just because you have an expert involved with your custody case does not mean that she will have to testify. Sometimes the judge is sufficiently impressed by the report to indicate to the lawyers before the trial that the final decision will probably reflect its conclusions. Usually, whether or not the expert testifies depends upon the legal strategy. In certain cases, involving the expert in court makes a lot of sense; in other cases, it can be a waste of time and money. The parent should understand why the lawyer wants the expert to appear. Is it to expand upon the written report? To impress the judge with the expert's professionalism? Or, where the expert has recommended custody to the other side, is an appearance needed to challenge parts or all of the report?

In the custody case between Henry and Edith Swenson, the court-appointed child psychiatrist determined that Edith Swenson ought to have custody of Debbie, seven. After an extensive evaluation, Dr. Raj's opinion was that there was no evidence Edith was an unfit mother, as the father had charged. However, since it was clear that father and daughter had a warm and comfortable relationship, the report recommended that Henry should have extensive and unobstructed visitation.

Edith Swenson's lawyer was quite satisfied with these conclusions and had no plans to ask Dr. Raj to appear in court. But Mr. Frankel, the lawyer representing Mr. Swenson, did ask the doctor to testify. He told him that he did not wish to meet with him beforehand, and warned him: "When I have you on the witness stand, I'm going to make you aware of certain information that you didn't have during your evaluation. I think this additional information will cause you to change your mind."

Dr. Raj had to wait until the court date to find out what Mr. Frankel had in store for him. But once Dr. Raj took the witness stand, it turned out that there was actually no new information at all. So in spite of intense questioning by Mr. Frankel, Dr. Raj did not alter his opinion. The moral of this tale is to be sure you understand why your lawyer is asking the expert to testify. Make sure that the testimony can enhance your position and clarify certain issues for the judge. Otherwise, you could damage your case. Surely the judge now looked upon Mr. Frankel with a jaundiced eye, for the court's time had been wasted.

□ PREPARING YOUR CHILD □

In certain situations, depending upon the child and the inclination of the judge, the court may wish to speak with your child alone in chambers, *in camera,* as it is called. Judges often do this in order to meet the child themselves and draw their own conclusions. They may ask your child questions relating to his relationship with you and the other parent. Sometimes a judge may even ask the child directly with whom he would like to live. Of course, a judge will give greater weight to the wishes of a child of ten or older than to those of a four- or five-year-old. Some judges are quite comfortable talking to little children; others find it difficult. Those who are particularly concerned may attend special seminars to learn how to interview children in such situations; others have no specialized training and simply fly by the seat of their robes.

If the judge asks to meet your child *in camera,* it would be a good idea for you to prepare your son or daughter for this experience. Most children—even four-year-olds—know what a judge does and that it is important to be as honest as one can be when speaking to one. When talking about her parents' ongoing litigation, one nine-year-old said: "I'd like to talk to the judge myself. I could tell her how tired I am of always being in the middle. I want my mother and father to stop fighting. I would tell the judge the truth, the whole truth, and nothing but the truth!"

You might be surprised to find out that your child is so willing to see the judge while you yourself are so anxious about going to court. Children can be amazing in this way. They may show no fear in situations that leave adults trembling. Part of this, of course, is because younger children do not understand the complexities of certain situations or the consequences of behavior. Totally absorbed in their own way of seeing the

world, they may welcome the opportunity to speak with someone in authority whom they see as being completely fair and
good. To a child, the judge can represent a way to a resolution
of the conflict. The child doesn't perceive the judge as you or
your lawyer might—that is, as helpful to your side because she
herself went through a divorce, as promother or profather, as
biased in favor of joint custody, as impatient, long-winded,
and so on. For the child, the judge is simply a fair person who
can offer some relief.

It is for this reason that you need to take care in preparing
your child for the meeting with the judge. Be sure that you
give him permission to tell the truth. Don't set the agenda;
don't ask him to convey any messages to the judge. By all
means tell him you will be proud if he simply tells how he feels.
Even if you believe you are justified, resist coaching your child
for this interview. By doing so, you risk heightening his anxiety about his loyalties and about his own security. Judges, by
the way, are often wise when it comes to recognizing parental
manipulation. When five-year-old Ronnie Slater recited this
tale to Judge Markowitz—"I want to get rid of my father. He's
no good. He's never nice to me, and I never have any fun with
him"—she knew at once that Ronnie had been coached by his
mother. Judge Markowitz had read the expert's report, which
indicated that Ronnie enjoyed spending time with his father.
The judge also knew children of this age in this situation hardly
ever talk that way. They are, she knew, usually attached to
both of their parents.

You can also let your child know that he does not have to
tell you what he has told the judge. This could make the child
feel more comfortable about the interview and free him to
speak more openly.

Sometimes, however, a child will resist the private interview
with the judge and express panic at the thought of it. Here you
will have to use your judgment. The whole point is to minimize the potential for psychological harm. If it seems that the
child cannot be consoled and reassured, then the *in camera* interview should not be required. It would be proper for an expert

—or the lawyer—to notify the judge that such a child could be harmed by the interview. In most cases, it is not crucial for the judge to hold this session.

Aside from the *in camera* interview, your child may be quite curious and interested about what else will happen during the trial. Most children will not ask to attend. However, if your child wants to go, ask him why he wants to be there. Is he just curious? Is he worried about you? Does he want to make sure the judge is fair? By asking questions, you can learn your child's hidden agenda in wanting to attend. You should tell your child that the court is for grown-ups only, but that when you come home, you'll tell him about it.

For many young children, the actual trial is frightening and may be perceived as the time when they will lose one or both parents. An older child will have a better idea of what goes on in court from watching films and television. But children of any age can be expected to be anxious about this event, and will look to you for guidance. Now is the time to reinforce how much both parents love them and will always be involved in their lives. In comforting your children in this way, you can also comfort yourself.

□ PREPARING YOURSELF □

And what of your own preparation? Your lawyer will, of course, meet with you before the trial to go over technical aspects of courtroom procedure, to outline strategy, and to discuss how you will participate. Like the expert witness, you should work with him to anticipate questions from the opposing side. Preparing in this way will help reduce the anxiety you are bound to feel. And certainly you and your lawyer will review all the questions he will be asking you when you testify. This is permissible and necessary so that you can be as prepared as possible. And the more active a role you take in the preparation of your testimony, the better you will feel. If you have difficulty with a certain question or don't like the way your lawyer poses it, speak up! If you think there is something you should be asked that he doesn't seem to be covering, speak up again! If your lawyer's style is brusque or otherwise distasteful to you, resist any inclination to stay silent.

You need to remember, though, that different lawyers have different courtroom styles; some present their case in a reasonable, restrained, and methodical manner; others go straight for the jugular. You may be able to modulate your own lawyer's approach when he questions you, but be prepared to find yourself in court listening to someone you are paying mount a full-scale attack on the character of the person with whom you once pledged to spend the rest of your life. Such an experience can be profoundly shocking and depressing. It's hard not to feel like a failure: for whatever reasons, you and the other parent were not able to stay together or even reach a settlement on parting. Now, outside forces seem to be in control. You must put your faith in the competence of your lawyer and your hope in the fairness and objectivity of the judge.

JUST BEFORE A custody case is heard in court, parents may harbor a number of worries they feel uneasy about bringing up with their lawyers. No matter how embarrassed you might feel about asking certain questions, it is better to say whatever is on your mind to reduce your stress as much as possible as well as to prevent an issue from suddenly exploding. Here are some typical questions and responses.

1. Will my wife's/husband's lawyer attack me in court?

Unfortunately, even if your spouse has no intention of trying to accuse or embarrass you, his or her lawyer may do so. If you are on the witness stand, the opposing lawyer may ask questions designed to rattle you—about your past or present sex life, for example, or about some actual (or fabricated) skeleton in your closet. The question could be something completely unexpected, like "Have you ever spent time in jail?" Your lawyer will surely object, and the judge may even admonish the opposing lawyer against any more such questions. You, however, may be shaken and put on the defensive, and your subsequent testimony could suffer. So be prepared for questions designed to throw you off guard. Wait a beat or two after they are asked so that your lawyer has a chance to object. Try not to become angry, arrogant, or sarcastic with the opposing lawyer. No matter what, do not lose your temper. If there is any kind of past indiscretion or secret that could be used against you in court, by all means discuss it beforehand with your lawyer so you can prepare a strategy for dealing with it in case it does come up.

2. What will the room be like?

Courtrooms vary in appearance, from comfortable and modern to dark and foreboding. A visit to your local courthouse prior to your court date can help to relieve some of your anxiety about being in unfamiliar surroundings. Often, although the courtroom may be large, it will contain only a few people on the day of your hearing: the principals on both sides, the judge, and the court reporter. You may feel very small and forlorn. The judge sits up front, above everyone else; he or she may be wearing judicial robes. There may be the state and American flags on either side of the bar; perhaps some inscription on the woodwork above. Everything is designed to maximize the sense of awe and even fear that should come with respect for the law. You may be sitting just a few yards from your spouse, separated by lawyers and some space between the tables. It can seem very strange to sit so close to people and yet act as if they aren't there. Sometimes, people not connected with your case may be sitting in the courtroom; they could be from another case, or members of the general public out for some entertainment. If you are a celebrity or are well known in your community, you and your lawyer should anticipate the presence of the press, and plan how to respond to any questions.

3. *What should I wear?*

Your lawyer will probably tell you to dress conservatively. Men should wear suits or jackets and ties. A dark color is probably preferable. Women should plan to dress in a conservative outfit and in subdued colors. They should dress as they would for a job interview. It is important to present yourself in a way that is comfortable for you. You should not be acting out a role but presenting your true self. If that true self is most comfortable in jeans or a floor-length gown, however, it should be moderated to fit the occasion.

4. *How long will the trial last?*

You may be disappointed to learn that your trial could take a long time to complete; it may take a week, but several weeks is not unusual. Some judges try to effect a settlement even during the trial, and may ask the lawyers to go back to their clients with a new proposal and then return to court in a few weeks. There may be a delay until an expert witness is able to schedule time to testify, or any number of postponements for various technical reasons (or the judge might be going on vacation!) Whatever the cause, you can be sure the trial will take longer than you expected. Unfortunately, there is little you can do about this.

5. *Once the trial starts, can we still reach a settlement?*

As we noted above, judges try to get both sides to settle up to the bitter end. If you have an idea you think might appeal to the other side, by all means have your lawyer propose it if it fits into his legal strategy. Most lawyers would like to reach a settlement that leaves both sides feeling like winners, rather than risk the possibility of losing the case. Conversely, if the other side presents a proposal during the trial, keep an open mind and discuss it with your lawyer.

6. *Is there anything to keep in mind when I am testifying?*

Yes. In general, keep your answers short and to the point. If the question asked is a yes–or–no question, answer simply yes or no; do not elaborate on your answers unless specifically asked to do so. If you do not know something, say so. The cross-examining lawyer may bring up some aspect of your parenting of which you are not proud. For example, she may question you about something nasty you said about the other parent in front of the child. She might refer to a time when you lost your temper with your child and scolded him severely, or even smacked him on the backside. You will present a far more impressive picture of yourself if you own up to these things rather than denying them, and then go on to say that you regret them, that you did lose your temper and that you will do your best not to have it happen again. The point is that you make a better witness if you come across as a human being. That is of far greater interest to the judge than your trying to portray yourself as the perfect parent.

7. *What if I don't like the way my lawyer is handling the case in court?*

Discuss your concerns immediately with him, but don't speak out in the courtroom! You may object to a line of questions your lawyer is following, or he may be leaving something out. Bring this to his attention during a break, or ask him to request a brief recess if the matter is truly urgent.

8. *What role does the judge play during the trial?*

The judge makes sure that the trial is being conducted according to the law, that lawyers' questions are legitimate, and that the rights of all those involved are being protected. While the judge is the decisionmaker, he is also very much a part of the process of the trial. Judges often ask their own questions; they might ask a witness to clarify something or they may raise

159

a whole new area of interrogation that they feel was not adequately covered by either lawyer. Be prepared for this kind of direct questioning from the judge and answer these questions just as you would those from the lawyers. Be sure to be respectful. Address the judge as "Your Honor," or "Judge." This is not the place to get angry or lose your temper, no matter what questions are asked.

9. What is the judge looking for?

The judge is looking for a relatively stable adult who has a deep psychological bond and a consistent nurturing history with the child, and who demonstrates the best overall plan for the child's future. The judge is not looking for a parent who can provide the longest list of what is wrong with the other parent.

10. Do all judges work the same way?

No. Some judges ask a lot of questions of the witnesses and parents as well as the experts. Others let the lawyers do this. Some judges encourage children to speak with them *in camera;* many do not. Some insist that the expert witness send the report of the evaluation only to them. Others don't mind if lawyers (and possibly parents) also receive copies. Some judges, by words and decisions, show definite ideas or biases about joint custody, father custody, homosexual parents, etc. Others remain quite open to the special circumstances of each case. It is up to your lawyer to decide how best to deal with this.

11. How will I feel after going to court?

You can expect to feel any or all of the following: exhausted, drained, anxious, frightened, angry, frustrated, apprehensive, hopeful, elated, confused, uncertain, and numb! A day in court is an intense and fatiguing experience. You will have paid close attention to all the proceedings all day, and if you have testified, you can expect to be even more tired.

TAKE GOOD CARE of yourself at this time. Relax when you get home. Minimize any other stress. Eat well. If you can, take your mind off the day by seeing a movie, visiting friends, or watching television. Do not drown your sorrow and anxiety in alcohol. If the trial is continuing the next day, by all means go to bed early. Avoid sleeping pills if you can; otherwise you won't be at your best in the morning.

If your day in court is over and the trial has ended, the next step in the process is the handing down of the judge's decision. But as you will see in the next chapter, this step too can be as slow as so many of the others in the long set of procedures that make up the custody dispute.

THE DECISION

THERE IS HARDLY anything more dramatic than the handing down of a judicial decision. We have all seen movies and plays with a climactic courtroom scene that keeps everyone on the edge of their seats. In your custody dispute, the denouement is of a different sort. First, there is no jury, no foreman who stands up to announce your fate and the fate of your family. Instead, the decision rests with just one person: the judge. Second, you may not learn about the decision for days or even weeks after the trial has ended. Your lawyer may tell you by phone, by mail, or in person. Or you may receive some kind of notice from the court itself. In any case, the paradox of a custody trial decision is that there is extreme tension even in the seeming lack of drama. You wait, as you have waited for so long. And your child continues to suffer uncertainty and confusion.

You and your lawyer should not forget that a small child's sense of time and the future is not as developed as yours. To your child, two weeks or a month can seem like forever. And while there may be considerable contact between lawyer and client even during this waiting period, the child is still excluded. Yet the longer the delay, the greater his confusion and anxiety about the outcome. Be sure you remain sensitive to your child's sense of time as you wait through this difficult period. Be there for him even as you deal with your own pain.

□ IF YOU'RE THE "WINNER" □

Even though you have learned in this book that nobody—least of all a child—wins in a custody dispute, the adversarial system tells you otherwise. After the judge hands down the decision, one parent wins the case and the other loses. But both will experience complicated feelings and respond in many different ways to the news.

The parent who wins the custody case has a number of emotional reactions. The first is often an intense feeling of relief. The winning parent thinks about the years of litigation, the psychological upheavals, and the present victory: "Now I have won the right to my child. He is safe with me. Although the court requires visitation, I am in charge here." The tension and anxiety that have become chronic throughout the long proceedings lift, and the parent begins to feel hopeful again. Joy accompanies relief. A parent who has been afraid of actually losing a child now feels that this most dreaded of possibilities will not happen. A parent whose "whole life is my child" is reassured. A father who wins custody of his son feels happy the judge has decided that fathers and sons ought to be together; he can now go on to raise the boy the way he has always wanted to—without interference from the mother. A mother might feel the same way about winning custody of a daughter. The winning parent always believes the judge has made the correct decision and the expert witness appointed by the court is the fairest and best of all child experts.

Along with relief and joy, the victorious parent feels intense pride at having been successful. The judge has acknowledged that he or she is the better parent and therefore more fit to take care of the child or children. There is no need to feel shame. All the terrible things said in courtroom testimony and in the legal papers have proved to be lies and exaggerations. This parent can now feel proud to visit the child's school, the doctor's office, the community library, the recreation center. The winning parent's self-esteem is restored and enhanced. Parents who win custody suits also often feel that now they will be more respected by their own parents. Most important of all, the parent feels vindicated in the eyes of the child, for that child can now look up to him or her and be reassured that his needs will be met.

As well as feeling pride and relief, the successful parent may experience more negative emotions, particularly resentment or a desire for vengeance. These emotions may surface only later, and the parent may not be fully aware of the depth of the hostility. This parent may feel the judge didn't go far enough, and want the other, "defeated" parent to be stripped of all power over the family, have zero contact with the child, and disappear forever. According to this fantasy, the "bad" parent, who made life so miserable for the family, now deserves to be punished.

Desire for revenge may also lead to feelings of guilt, as may winning itself. In the midst of elation and relief, the victorious parent may worry about the mental and physical health of the other parent. Perhaps at one point, in the heat of the dispute, a mother threatened suicide if she did not win custody. The ex-husband who has been awarded custody now worries that this may happen. There is guilt for what the children have suffered as well. A parent sees a previously healthy child angry, frustrated, anxious or perhaps displaying some alarming behavior, and feels responsible, even if he or she also believes that the litigation was necessary. Perhaps this parent refused to participate in mediation, or in working out a joint custody arrangement. Such guilt is understandable and normal, given the circumstances.

Very often, the mixture of emotions the successful parent experiences leads to anxiety and self-doubt. "Did the judge make the right decision after all? Am I really the better parent, and will I be equal to the task of caring for my child? Will I still get help from the other parent? Will our child forgive us for having engaged in this battle? Will the child be all right? Will I be able to lead a fulfilling life of my own, separate from being the sole custodial parent? Will there be relitigation later on? What will the future bring?"

The successful parent may thus experience emotions toward the child and the losing parent that range from magnanimous to hostile. Positive behaviors include offering the olive branch to the former adversary, being generous with the visitation schedule, and not interfering with visits. Operating from a position of power, the winning parent is often able to reduce the level of anxiety and hostility and to begin the healing process for the whole family. If all goes well, this parent will now be able to get on with the job of parenting, liberated from the legal shackles that have burdened both parents during the litigation.

The Doyles, even while engaged in a custody dispute over their eleven-year-old daughter, Maria, still lived in the same house. They had gone beyond shouting at each other and had been using the "silent treatment" for months. The house was filled with tension, and Maria was trying hard to relate to each of them as if there were no problem. But the pretense wasn't working. She was very distressed throughout the litigation. Some nights, when she had dinner at home with just her father, she felt guilty that she was hurting her mother.

One of the brightest students at her school, Maria's grades had suffered. Although four months in psychotherapy had eased her worst fears, she felt relief only at the end of the legal case. Her mother was named sole custodial parent, and the house was sold. As tensions abated, Alice Doyle encouraged her daughter to spend more time with her father. She told Maria that she regretted the fighting and realized how important it was for Maria to see her father on a regular basis. She wanted Maria to know that it was really all right to stay over at her father's new home. Alice Doyle's willingness to put aside her anger at her former husband helped Maria come to terms with her parents' divorce and their antagonism during the custody dispute.

But not all parents who gain sole custody are able to put aside rage at their former spouse. Cheryl Pierce was one who could not; she was still furious at Edward Pierce months after the divorce and custody dispute were over. She persisted in believing that it was he alone who had caused the family to break up, by being lazy around the house and staying out late with his friends. Cheryl suspected that Edward had had several affairs during their ten-year marriage, although she had never been able to prove it.

The Pierces' son, Larry, was now eight years old. He had been going through the process of his parents' divorce and the ensuing custody dispute since he was five. During that very important time in his life, Larry had lived with his mother; his father had had an apartment a half-hour's drive away. The arrangement was that Larry was to see his father one day a week and on alternate weekends, staying overnight on Saturdays. But Edward Pierce was often away, or else, according to his ex-wife, would cancel the visits at the last minute.

Cheryl Pierce had not hesitated to tell Larry how much she despised his father. "He's just no good," she would tell him. "You don't need him, anyway. You have me and Grandma and Grandpa. We're your family." Cheryl justified this by saying, "I don't want to lie to my son. Why should I pretend that I still like and respect the man? I want Larry to know the truth about his father: the man is a bum. He has a job, all right, but he's still a bum, and a liar to boot."

After custody was finally decided in her favor, Cheryl was even more reluctant to involve her ex-husband in Larry's life. Now *she* began to cancel the visits, often at the last minute. Or she would plan not to be around when Edward came to visit his son. She would have her father intercept her ex-husband: "Larry doesn't want to go with you," the grandfather would say to Edward Pierce. "I think you should go away and try again some other time." Larry would hear all this and become quite upset. Sometimes, in tears, he would then tell his father to go away. But Cheryl Pierce's revenge backfired, because Edward returned to court to secure his rights of visitation. Eight-year-old Larry, of course, suffered the most. Those winning parents who can give up such impulses for vengeance toward their ex-mates not only free themselves to go on with their own lives, they liberate their children as well.

□ IF YOU'RE THE ''LOSER'' □

Parents who lose a custody dispute also experience complex feelings. There is certainly a pervasive sadness and a great sense of loss. Unless they are determined to relitigate, these parents know that their relationship with the child has now forever changed. The losing parents feel second-rate, as if they will no longer matter very much in the child's life. A mourning process —not unlike the one that occurs at the death of a loved one— begins. For many parents, it feels as if a part of them has died. The mourning is for the loss of the relationship with the child as well as for the marriage. As in any mourning, the parent feels devastated, frightened, confused, and profoundly sad. Over time, however, most parents will adjust to a new life and begin the process of healing and redefining the relationship with the child, although some handle the process better than others.

After a bitter custody dispute in another country, Mark Kaplan, his ex-wife, Judy, and their eight-year-old son moved back to the United States. Judy had lost custody, but her lawyer told her to consider relitigating the case upon her return to the States. "International custody cases can be so complicated," he told her, "and you just might win back home." Judy thought about this. It was tempting. But she also considered what the effect of the custody fight had been on her son: he was going to need psychological counseling. She and Mark had worked out a very liberal visitation arrangement. She had agreed to abide by the foreign court's decision. Back in the United States, Judy Kaplan decided not to pursue further litigation, and to make the best of an unhappy situation.

For a minority of parents, however, the loss of custody can lead to a clinical depression. (Fathers in particular may be prone to this kind of reaction, especially if they have suffered a depression in the past or have a family history of this disorder.) For these parents, the loss is magnified and intensified. Normal daily functioning stops. They are not able to sleep or to go to work. They lose their appetite, their sex drive, and their self-esteem. They may even become suicidal. Such extreme reactions are rare but they do occur, and when they do, they require medical intervention.

The majority of parents who lose custody of their children do not become clinically depressed, but all are sad and many are angry. They feel enraged at the ex-spouse and betrayed by the legal system. They perceive the judge as having been misled by the other side and as inadequate to the task of seeing justice served. They also resent the lawyers, as well as others in the community whom they regard as having let them down: teachers, the doctor, perhaps a clergyman, neighbors, babysitters. Some may even be angry at the children, and regard them as the cause of all their misery.

Parents who lose custody often experience fear as well, fear that the child will now be kept from them, that they will be forever embarrassed by this legal decision, that their life will always seem meaningless and empty, that they will never be happy again. Fear, in turn, can lead to feelings of desperation and the desire for revenge. Such parents feel that unless they do something soon, their life (and perhaps the children's as well) will be ruined by the court decision.

The feelings of the losing parent often lead to behaviors that may be detrimental to the child. The parent may choose to avoid coping with the sense of loss by withdrawing from the child's life. This might be manifested in less frequent visits, last-minute cancellations, or repeated instances of "forgetting" scheduled visits. Alternately, while on a visit with the child, this parent might behave in a particularly passive manner, or might arrange it so that the presence of other people will dilute the relationship with the child. An astute child probably will recognize such behavior for what it is; other children, unfortunately, will be more likely to feel hurt or angry because of the curtailed time with the parent.

After failing to receive sole custody of his twin girls, Vincent Poletti launched a campaign of harassment against his ex-wife. He delayed child support payments or deliberately sent the wrong amount. He arrived for his scheduled visits early, late, or not at all. He often told his seven-year-old daughters that their mother was "a great actress" and "a liar," and that she had fooled everyone: her lawyer, the court-appointed psychiatrist, and the judge. Mr. Poletti just couldn't accept the decision.

Occasionally, feelings of desperation and loss lead a parent to kidnap the child, (as we noted in chapter 8). While kidnapping often succeeds in taking the child away from the legal custodial parent, it exacts a terrible toll: enormous stress for *both* parents and child. In addition, it prevents the family from dealing with the profound feelings that follow the court decision.

□ LIVING WITH THE DECISION □

After your custody dispute has been decided, you may be surprised by the complexity of your feelings, and perhaps even by some of your behavior. You may have thought that with the judge's decision would come peace of mind and a clear head. But whether you find yourself the winner or the loser, you are by no means at peace. What can you do?

If you have won custody, acknowledge to yourself that your feelings are very complicated right now. Allow yourself to feel the full range of emotions, from elation to revenge. You don't have to act upon any of these feelings, but experiencing them is the first step toward sorting them out. Resist the temptation to take revenge on the other parent; it will serve no good purpose and will cause your child further hurt. As you begin to calm down and to think about the future, recognize that your ex-spouse will continue to play an important role in your child's future. It will be very destructive to the child for you to behave as if this parent no longer exists.

Begin to plan for your ex-spouse's involvement so that you can reach some equilibrium. It is never too early to sit down with the other parent and work out specific plans for their future connection with your child and with you. Take some time to imagine what the losing parent is going through. Now is an excellent time for you to show as much empathy as you can. This may be more difficult for you than displaying anger, but it will be far more fruitful for your family in the long run.

If you have lost the dispute, don't take any specific action for a while. You too need to acknowledge all your complicated emotions. Allow yourself to feel them. If you do take any action out of the fear or anger you are feeling, you may regret it later, for by acting in the heat of emotion now you may threaten your future relationship with your child. While it is understandable that you may have fantasies about snatching your child away and disappearing, don't do it! There is no victory in that for you, and you can end up in serious legal difficulties. If you find yourself becoming more and more upset and think you may be clinically depressed, see a mental health professional. It will be important now for you to know you have an ally you can trust.

If you have lost your suit, by all means be sure to discuss

your options with your lawyer. Losing custody does not mean having your parental rights terminated. The legal system still recognizes you as a very important part of your child's life. Your rights of visitation will be protected by the court, should the other side attempt to sabotage them. You have the right to be involved by the school in your child's academic life. You have the right to vacations or extended visits with your child. If the custodial parent wants to move away with your child, you have the right to seek relief in the courts if you do not feel this move is in your child's best interests.

If your former partner does express the desire to have a reasonable relationship with you, by all means do your part, if you can. In doing so, you will be an immense help to your child as she or he begins to put the custody dispute in the past.

□ THE IMPACT ON THE CHILD □

How will the judge's decision affect your child? As with so many other aspects of your child's life, your son or daughter's reaction will very much depend upon your own. Be sure that the child will scrutinize your reactions, listen to your words, watch your facial expressions and mirror your moods at this time. A younger child (before the preteen years) will be more concerned with your reaction to the decision than with the actual decision itself. A child of six or seven is not going to understand the ramifications of your having been awarded sole or joint custody, or the fact that you lost a legal case. But if you react to the decision with rage, anxiety, or intense fear, your child will respond the same way. If you experience a profound sense of loss, if you panic, if you become depressed and withdrawn, then your child—especially if he or she has been living with you—will share these emotions. If you react with more equanimity (whether as a winner or a loser) and are able to recognize that life will go on, albeit differently, then your child will react the same way. Remember that for a younger child, the issue has never been winning or losing but rather, "Will I still be taken care of? Will both my parents still love me?"

Whether you have won the case or not, there are appropriate ways to transmit this news to your child. First, it is important that you let the child know the decision was made for all of you by the judge. Even a very young child can understand this, and it will help as you begin to explain things in detail. Your son or daughter will realize that the outcome was determined by some other authority. This is important whether or not you are to be the sole custodial parent. If you have won, telling your child that the decision came from the judge, not you, lessens the danger of her seeing you as all-powerful. A child of four or five might think: "If you got rid of Daddy, you could get rid of me too." Being clear about who decided will make you seem less frightening in your child's eyes. Moreover, if it was not you who decided the outcome, she will not be angering you by remaining attached to the other parent. If the court has awarded you custody, let your child know that although she will live with you, she will see the other parent regularly.

What is *not* appropriate is for you to explain the custody decision by asserting that you have been judged to be the better parent, that the judge was very smart to realize this, or that now your child needs only one parent: you. Otherwise intelligent people have been known to indulge in this kind of damaging behavior as they gloat over their courtroom victory.

Do tell your child that the judge also decided what the best living arrangements would be, and that he wants her to have regular contact with both parents. Emphasize that the judge knows both parents love the child and wants both to be full-time parents to her. Say that both of you will always be involved with her, even though you will not all be living together as you were before.

If you are the noncustodial parent, you also need to be able to offer some explanation to the child. You too will need to explain that the decision was the judge's and not yours. You must assure the child that although she will live with your ex-spouse, you will remain deeply involved with her life. You will have to resist the temptation to tell your child that the judge was stupid, or that the other parent lied and fooled the judge; you will have to control the urge to engage in other self-serving behaviors precipitated by disappointment and anger. You may very well be angry, but it is unfair to try to use your child as an ally. A child cannot possibly understand the complexity of the situation, and you will be placing a heavy and unfair burden upon your child if you persist in confiding in her.

But even if you are both extremely careful in your conversations with your child, you cannot prevent the decision from having a strong impact on her. Just as it will change your lives, so it will change your child's. Certainly the kind of parenting she receives will be very different from what she knew when the family was intact. But there will be other changes as well. Over the coming months and years, your child will face changes in such areas as finances, schooling, and possibly even where she lives.

Under the court-directed living arrangement, your child may become aware of financial pressures. If there is to be a change in schools, it means making new friends and getting used to new teachers. The custody decision might also require the child to move to a new home, possibly in a new neighborhood. You will need to be as sensitive to all these changes as you can. By granting a child the emotional space and time to become accustomed to the postdecision arrangements, you will be helping her to resolve the situation for herself.

MOST PROFESSIONALS WHO work closely with families agree that the primary factors in a child's postcustody adjustment are continuing relationships with both parents, the quality of those relationships, and the quality of the postdivorce relationship between the parents. Many parents lose sight of the guiding dynamic that so vitally affects the postdivorce life of children: the better your relationship with the other parent, the less tension there will be for your child. Reasonable ex-spouses can often work out problems if they make the child's best interests their priority.

Dorothy and Alex Bolton had litigated a custody dispute concerning their two sons, Fred, ten, and Dennis, eight. The family had been evaluated by a court-appointed child psychiatrist, Dr. Richard Galter, who had recommended that Dorothy Bolton have sole custody. The judge had so ruled. One issue Alex Bolton had raised during the dispute was his concern that Dorothy was often too harsh and punitive when she disciplined the boys. Alex was afraid that they would grow up fearful and under the shadow of real or threatened punishment if their mother were the sole custodial parent. Dorothy had admitted that she was inclined to be too much of a disciplinarian. She promised that she would make more of an effort to restrain her authoritarian tendencies, and agreed that if she felt she needed advice, she would call Dr. Galter.

About seven months after the custody decision was handed down, Alex called Richard Galter. Although the doctor's opinion had been that Mrs. Bolton should be the custodial parent, Alex Bolton believed that Dr. Galter had been fair and impartial in his evaluation of the family. He trusted the doctor and was calling this time for his advice. Alex said he had received a disturbing letter from eight-year-old Dennis. The child had written that his mother was always yelling at him, punishing him, and occasionally slapping him across the face. The letter ended: "Daddy, please come and get me. I want to live with you, not Mommy. She treats me real bad. And don't tell her about this letter because I know she will hit me."

Mr. Bolton had immediately called his lawyer, who suggested that he first talk to Dr. Galter. The child psychiatrist recommended that Mr. Bolton call his ex-wife to invite her to a joint session with the psychiatrist. That way they could discuss this issue on neutral ground and, it was hoped, resolve the problem without placing Dennis in the middle. The therapist cautioned Mr. Bolton not to assume that Dennis's letter was entirely accurate. Dorothy agreed to come for the session. With some guidance from the therapist, she and Alex were able to discuss the letter calmly and without attacking each other. Dr. Galter explained to both of them how a young child might distort certain facts to pit one parent against the other and to get them involved with each other again—even in a negative way. Alex believed Dorothy when she explained that she never actually slapped Dennis but had made a threatening gesture when she had just run out of patience. For Dennis, she now realized, the threat was as real as the deed. She spoke with Dr. Galter about other ways of disciplining her child, and Alex was supportive. Both parents worked out a common strategy and checked with Dr. Galter as they put it into practice.

Once divorced parents can put the custody dispute in perspective, many of them will realize that the court decision is just that—a decision, and nothing more. It is the closing of one chapter and the opening of another. It is not a guide for living for the family or even a guarantee that things will work out happily for everyone. It is just the best the judge can do at the time, given the facts as they have been presented. Now everyone in the family must begin a new life. But what kind of life is up to you. The actual legal decision means little to your children. What they want is the assurance of a deep, continuing relationship with both parents and the knowledge that you love them and want to be close to them as well. Given this wisdom and understanding, former partners who have dissolved their own bonds can invigorate and nurture those that connect them to their children as everyone begins to recover from the wounds of the dispute. The next chapter, on visitation, explores these issues from a more practical perspective.

VISITATION

THE JUDGE WILL usually address the issue of visitation as part of the overall custody decision. The recommendations of the court-appointed expert witness who has evaluated the family frequently form the basis for the specific arrangement, although sometimes judges come up with their own visitation plans. The details can, of course, vary. For example, the child may see the noncustodial parent for an overnight visit during the week and on alternate weekends. Or the child may visit with the parent without an overnight during the week but will stay overnight every Saturday. Supervised visitation, in which a third pertson is present when a child visits a parent can also be ordered by the court. That third person may be a family member trusted by both parents or someone appointed by the court, such as a social worker or childcare worker. Supervised visitation usually occurs if a judge belives the noncustodial parent may say or do something inappropriate that could harm the child or increase tensions between the parents.

Many divorcing parents are not aware that the award of sole custody to one does not terminate the parental rights of the other. Nor does it in any way provide legal justification for impeding or attempting to sever the child's relationship with that parent. Most judges will enforce visitation orders if they are being ignored. Sometimes they will even threaten to reverse their decision and award custody to the noncustodial parent if the custodial parent has denied access to the child. A judge's intentions in such a situation may well be to protect the child's best interests, but the effects of an abrupt reversal of custody (especially if mediation or parental counseling has not been tried first) can be extremely disruptive and detrimental to the child's welfare. Do your best to avoid this crisis.

What is the purpose of visitation, and why is it so important? Visitation provides children with the opportunity to maintain continuity in their relationship with the parent with whom they no longer primarily live. If this relationship is rewarding and nurturing, and does not compromise the child's health and safety, maintaining it will be extremely important to the child's psychological development. For although you and your ex-spouse have decided that you can never be reconciled, and even if you feel intense rage and frustration at each other, your child will never see things in quite the same way. As Sonja Goldstein and Albert J. Solnit put it in their valuable guide, *Divorce and Your Child*: "Your child is not the one who got the divorce and should neither have to lose contact with one parent as a result of it nor be burdened, especially as he gets older, with an inflexible visitation schedule."[1]

Once you are able to accept your child's independent role in the new situation, you should welcome visitation with the non-custodial parent as an opportunity for both child and parent to maintain their connection as well as a chance to have some respite from parenting. If, on the other hand, you balk at visitation or make it difficult, remember that you run the risk of further psychological harm to the child. The removal of one parent from the life of the child because the parents have been unable to set up a visitation arrangement is a profound loss. The child will experience this loss in a number of ways, including feeling sad, confused, uncertain, and anxious. Even an infant or toddler will feel the loss and change in routine. It might be expressed as a mood change, or sleep or appetite disturbances. A young child of five or six will often feel somehow responsible for the loss and experience it as a punishment for some real or imagined misdeed. An older child will feel betrayed and angry. To minimize the chances for harm, this chapter contains some guidelines to help you and your child with this part of your new life. But first we need to look at visitation from the child's perspective.

□ VISITATION FROM THE □ CHILD'S PERSPECTIVE

The resolution of a custody dispute, either by mediation or through the courts, most often brings relief to the child. Children are sometimes led by one parent to believe in a particular outcome, only to be told something else by the other parent, and the long delays in our legal process can aggravate and intensify their uncertainty. They can become confused, anxious, and angry, not knowing which parent they can trust, never feeling sure about where—or with whom—they will live. Children of any age can begin the readjustment and healing process only when they know what their living arrangements will be. The opportunity for regular visitation with the noncustodial parent is of paramount importance in this process. After a custody dispute, both parents are still under a great deal of emotional pressure. One parent may be happy with the visitation agreement; the other may have serious reservations. Rarely do parents in such a situation stop to reflect upon the experience from the child's point of view. Yet if parents would adopt this focus, most visitation problems could be prevented.

Children approach visitation with a number of complicated feelings. In general, the younger the child, the more difficult it is for that child to deal with all these feelings. The most serious —and most common—problem young children encounter is the desire to be with the noncustodial parent and the simultaneous wish not to offend or disappoint the custodial parent. Most children who have had a reasonably good relationship with a parent prior to the custody battle will want to maintain that relationship afterward. They will see visitation as a means of keeping contact, as reassurance that they are still loved by that parent, and as a stabilizing element in a chaotic family situation. After a custody dispute, a child is eager to reestablish stability and predictability. He looks forward to the visits and enjoys the ongoing connection with the parent whom he no longer sees every day.

On the other hand, children are also extremely cautious about offending the custodial parent. If tensions between the parents remain high, the child will naturally be aware of them, and they will certainly affect his feelings about visitation. Maintaining regular contact with the noncustodial parent helps mitigate a young child's fear of abandonment, but if the custodial parent is obviously unhappy about the visits, the child may in turn fear abandonment by the custodial parent and become extremely anxious and confused. This confusion is common in young children attempting to come to terms with their new family status, but it is also seen in older children, even years after the custody dispute has been settled. Parents who are sensitive to this dilemma will be best able to help their child negotiate these troubled waters.

Charlie Whitson, six years old, told his therapist that he did not wish to visit his father now that the judge had told him he would be living with his mother. Charlie said, "It's no fun at my father's. We never do anything. There aren't enough toys at his house, and we never play anything." But Dr. Ramona Walker's interviews with Mr. Whitson revealed that Charlie was exaggerating a great deal. Although his father did not have the same number of toys at his place that Charlie had at home with his mother, Mr. Whitson had set up a room just for Charlie in his new apartment and had bought quite a few toys. He and Charlie played with them regularly whenever Charlie visited.

Later in the therapy session, Charlie noticed a game on the therapist's toy shelf. "My dad has the same game at his house," Charlie said excitedly. "He taught me how to play it and now I can beat him. Let's play it now." Charlie then told the therapist more about what he and his father did together on visits. "Sometimes we just sit quietly together," he said. "I like that too." Charlie's eyes filled with tears.

Mrs. Whitson freely admitted to the therapist that she often wished Charlie's father "would just disappear. He was a pain when we were married, he made my life almost impossible during the custody dispute, and he's a thorn in my side today. Why should I hide my feelings from Charlie? I want him to know the truth about his father. And I have to be true to my own feelings. The man does not know *how* to play with a child. He didn't even have a separate room for the boy until about a month ago. He doesn't know the first thing about being a parent, and I'm supposed to see to it that Charlie visits with him every damn week. Charlie doesn't want to go, anyway. Can you blame him? Why should he have to?"

Mrs. Whitson had believed Charlie when he told her there was nothing to do at his father's place. It confirmed what she had always thought about her former husband. Mr. Whitson, on the other hand, was concerned that his son was "turning into a liar—just like his mother!"

In a session with both parents, Dr. Ramona Walker tried to explain that Charlie was torn between his mother and his father. She was able to report with confidence that he certainly enjoyed being with his father; it was far from being "no fun." But Charlie also felt a strong allegiance to his mother and was very aware of her intensely negative feelings about the visitation. He saw his mother as his primary parent, the only person who was really taking care of all his needs. He was afraid to upset her and took every precaution not to appear to be siding with his father. So he seemed to have adopted his mother's view of his father. The child was not intentionally lying, but rather was trying to tell his mother what he assumed she wanted to hear. Dr. Walker pointed out to each parent how their animosity was perpetuating anxiety in their child. She offered to meet with them for a few more sessions to try to improve the climate of visitation. They agreed, and the goal was accomplished.

□ HINTS FOR THE □ CUSTODIAL PARENT

After a dispute, the custodial parent often harbors the fantasy that with the "victory" will come peace and the exit of the noncustodial parent from the life of the child. The child will adapt quickly to having just one parent, and everything will work out at last. It's best to give up this kind of wishful thinking as soon as possible, and to remember that the child's ability to heal and rebound following a divorce and custody dispute is directly related to frequent and unimpeded access to *both* parents. You have to come to terms with this fact, and allow your understanding to inform your behavior toward your child and toward the noncustodial parent.

In considering visitation, the judge acts upon what he or she thinks is in your child's best interests. Even as the victorious parent, you may still be smarting from the unpleasant charges your ex-partner made against you in court. Yet now the judge has ordered visitation, and you are expected to comply without having any time to recover from the trauma of the custody battle. You are told that you must abide by the court's directions or risk serious penalties, which might even include a change in custody. Because of certain restrictions set down by the court regarding the visitation—such as the schedule you must follow, or a prohibition against your moving out of town with your children without court authorization—you might wonder whether you have won anything at all.

So be prepared. Just as your child will now experience all kinds of mixed feelings about the visitation, so will you. By acknowledging these complex feelings, you can help yourself (and your child) develop some equanimity about this next phase in your family life. The very first thing you must do is accept the fact that not only will visitation occur, but that it actually *needs* to occur for your child's welfare.

Your role in your child's visitation has three major aspects: how you prepare the child for the visit; how you conduct yourself during the visit; and how you behave when the child returns.

Here are some guidelines as you prepare for the visit: Do discuss the upcoming visit in a natural, relaxed way with your child. Do emphasize for her the fact that you realize how important these visits are. Do let her know that you will think about her while she is gone, but that you expect she will have a good time. Do indicate that you will be just fine while she is away and that you will have plenty to do.

Do *not* speak disparagingly about the noncustodial parent or indicate your displeasure with an upcoming visit. Do not give your child messages to relay to the other parent. Do not insist that she call you during the visit—unless that is something she wants to do. Do not ask her to provide you with a detailed schedule of what she expects to be doing with the other parent. Do not try to sabotage the visit by giving her subtle messages such as "Remember, you can come back as early as you like," or "If you and Daddy have a fight, just call me right away!" Do not imply that you will be lonely and sad while your child is away.

During the visit, no matter how much you may miss your child, fight the urge to make telephone calls to the other parent's house. These can be very disruptive to the visit, can cause undue stress to your child, and will almost certainly anger the other parent. Some parents make a habit of such calls, not realizing that they are unconsciously trying to upset the other parent. The inevitable result is that the child bears the burden of the stress.

Billy Hogan, six years old, visited his father every weekend. His mother would call him within minutes after his expected arrival at his father's house. "How are you, Billy?" she would ask. "Did Daddy drive there okay? He didn't go too fast, did he? You can tell Mommy." Billy enjoyed the visits with his father very much, but he also knew how they angered and upset his mother. Because he did not want to offend her, he sometimes called her after his arrival. On these occasions he would tell her that he was "bored"; sometimes he would cry and tell her how much he missed her. These calls only reinforced Mrs. Hogan's view of her former husband as an inadequate parent, and she never hid these feelings from Billy. The child became more and more anxious before, during, and after the visits; he began to wet his bed, and developed a fear of school.

Remember your child's intense vulnerability to your own feelings. Work out something reasonable with the other parent regarding telephone calls during a visit. Keep them to a minimum. Allow your child to visit unencumbered by worry about you and your concerns.

When the visit is over, receive the child as calmly and comfortably as you can. Try not to ignore the other parent or to behave as if he or she were invisible. Children are exquisitely sensitive to their parents' behavior during previsit and postvisit transitions. Their anxiety will be considerably lessened if they can observe their parents being civil with each other. Just a few words are sufficient. You certainly don't have to invite the other parent in for dinner!

Do not interrogate your child about the visit. Allow her to make the transition between homes without undue tension. She will need time to make the adjustment and to assimilate the visit. You should greet the child warmly, allow her to get settled, and then wait for things to unfold. Your child will appreciate the breathing space and will probably be more inclined to tell you about the visit than if you start interrogating her as she walks in the door. If you learn something worrisome about the other parent's behavior, take it up with the parent—*not* with the child. This may be difficult for you to do, but if you control yourself, you will remove your child from the center of any dispute, spoken or unspoken, that you might be having with the other parent.

□ HINTS FOR THE □ NONCUSTODIAL PARENT

If you are the noncustodial parent, you too may be harboring a great deal of ill will toward the other parent. Perhaps you are worried that the custodial parent will "brainwash" your child and convince him of your unworthiness. You may even be considering relitigation. All of these feelings can surface during visitation. If you are forced to deal with the other parent during the transitions between homes, your negative feelings might be almost too strong to control. Even so, it is important for you to do everything in your power to moderate these feelings so that the transitions can go smoothly. You may not be able to hide your feelings entirely from your child, but you should be civil and as low-key as possible when you pick him up. This is simply not the time to begin or continue an argument with the other parent.

As the noncustodial parent, do give your child time to adjust when he is with you. Indicate from time to time that you understand that it's sometimes hard to move from one household to another. Throughout the visit, show you recognize that your child has another life with the other parent, that it is okay with you, and that you still love him very much. Do make sure you can provide somewhere in your home which will be just for the child, so that he can become accustomed to having his own space. Do let him know that he is completely free to call the other parent, and that you will not be angry if he chooses to do so. Your child may need this communication as a way of assuring himself that the other parent will still be there for him upon his return. Do make sure that you plan activities at home as well as outside, that you prepare some meals at home, and that you frequently just "hang out" with your child, rather than always engaging in some activity. Do show an interest in his school, friends, and hobbies.

Janet Dickson, age ten, visited her father on alternate weekends and every Wednesday from 3 P.M. until school on Thursday morning. Mr. Dickson left work early on Wednesdays and picked up his daughter at school. Sometimes they went out to dinner, but most of the time Janet and her father cooked dinner together at his home. On Wednesdays, Janet did her homework, once in a while asking her father for help. On weekends, they did chores around the house, shopped, and often went to a museum or a movie. Sometimes they rented a videotape. Once in a while, Mr. Dickson had office work to do at home. For those few hours, Janet read, practiced piano, or talked on the phone to a friend. Mr. Dickson felt that his visits with Janet should be easy, natural, and no different in structure and activities from the normal family life they had shared before the breakup.

Do *not* interrogate your child about the other parent. If there are matters you believe you should know about, ask the parent directly. Don't turn your child into a messenger. Do not discuss court-related matters with him, if any are pending, unless he brings up the subject; in that case, be brief and neutral, and indicate that this is a matter for parents to decide. Do not become a "Disneyland parent," planning only action-packed, exciting activities to fill visits. This ploy may appeal to you as a way of getting back at your former spouse, but the result is not a victory. You'll create confusion and resentment in the child about the role of each parent; you might become the "good guy" and the other parent the disciplinarian. This will in turn create tension for the child when he is with the custodial parent, and the custodial parent's resentment will be passed back to him. Finally, do not make last-minute schedule changes when your child is supposed to return home. If he is due back at a certain time, respect that plan and stick to it!

At the conclusion of the visit, let your child know how much you enjoyed this visit and how much you are looking forward to the next one. If the schedule is set up in advance, you can tell him when the next visit will be. Do be civil with your ex-spouse when you return your child. Try to make this otherwise tense situation as easy as you can. Remember that although it may be difficult to maintain an ongoing relationship with the other parent, and although it may require all your emotional resources in the beginning even to talk to that person, the situation is even more difficult for the child. And easing the child's way should be your primary concern.

□ VISITATION TROUBLE □
POINTS

It is unlikely that visitation following a divorce will always proceed smoothly; following a custody dispute, it is bound to be a complicated affair. When tension is still high between parents after the court decision, each may look for a club with which to beat the other; each may seek proof that the other is unfit to be a parent. During visitation, parents will often suspect each other of not taking good care of the child, and accusations involving physical symptoms of illness will commonly surface at this time. It's important that you try to communicate positively with the other parent—there's still a good deal that you can do to correct and prevent trouble. Remember that a lot of what is going on may be fueled by feelings, not facts.

Carole Weber, five, visited her noncustodial father every other weekend. Although her mother felt she was too young to stay overnight, the judge who heard the custody case had ordered overnight visits. He had also indicated that he would be inclined to increase these overnight visits as Carole got older. The relationship between the parents was still quite tense, especially when Mr. Weber arrived to pick up his daughter. Occasionally, the Webers would argue in front of Carole, and Carole would cry.

Mr. Weber had a history of asthma and allergies in childhood, although he had rarely been plagued by them as an adult. After the custody dispute, however, it was Carole who developed mild asthma and sometimes broke out in a rash. She suffered symptoms such as wheezing, itchy and scaly skin, and sometimes, after visits with her father, hives. Louise Weber was furious with her former husband and accused him of "giving" these disorders to the child. She charged that he was not taking proper care of Carole during her visits, and that he was making her anxious; otherwise, she reasoned, the child would not be getting sick so often. Fortunately, Mrs. Weber agreed to meet with the court-appointed expert who had evaluated the family during the custody dispute. In the therapist's opinion, Carole was reacting to the tension between her parents—in this case by developing psychosomatic symptoms. The therapist told Mrs. Weber that children often develop such symptoms as they move from one parent's house to the other, especially if there is a high level of tension between the adults.

Once Mrs. Weber understood that Carole's disorders were a result of inevitable tensions—and not Mr. Weber's carelessness —her anxiety was allayed and she was able to moderate her own behavior out of concern for Carole's welfare. She decided not to return to court. Eventually, Carole's symptoms became less severe, though they remained chronic throughout her childhood.

In another case, a father accused his ex-wife of unfitness because, on visits with his infant daughter, he noted several times that she had diaper rashes. He took Polaroid snapshots of the rashes and compiled a dossier on the mother's alleged neglect of the child. A mother blamed her ex-husband for overfeeding their four-year-old son. She based her charge on the fact that the child would often vomit upon his return from a visit with his father.

Another mother was concerned because twice in the previous year, her eight-year-old son had been taken to a hospital emergency room during visits with his father. Once he had cut himself on some broken glass in a playground; on another occasion, he had run a high fever. This mother was convinced that her son was being neglected by her former husband. But parents in these situations should get all the facts before jumping to the conclusion that the other parent is unfit. It is important for parents to talk and share information. It's not so unusual for children to injure themselves enough to visit an emergency room or to vomit, run a high fever, or get a rash; these are common events in most children's lives and are usually the subject of family stories when the family stays together.

Some children may be quite nervous when they come home from a visit with a noncustodial parent. One mother told a child psychiatrist that whenever her six-year-old boy returned from a weekend with his father, he was "very hyper." As soon as he walked into the house, he would run up and down the stairs, tear in and out of all the rooms, get out some of his toys, abandon them for other toys, and repeatedly ask his mother if she was all right. His mother interpreted this behavior as a sign that the visits were not going well and that they were provoking great anxiety in her son. She suggested to the mediating therapist that the visits be curtailed.

But there are other interpretations and other solutions. Many young children display behavioral and even mild physical symptoms around visitation with the noncustodial parent. (The corresponding behavior changes in older children are usually less overt—often appearing as withdrawal or a desire to be "left alone" for a while.) In most cases, the symptoms result from the child's attempt to cope with the visitation in the context of ongoing conflict between the parents. A hyper child may be using extra movement to discharge the anxiety generated by the transition between his parents' homes rather than by the visit itself. Experienced therapists working with children involved in divorce and custody disputes know that although the visits themselves may go very well, the child will often show symptoms of distress afterward.

If you are the custodial parent and your child shows behavioral problems after a visit, try to understand what the behavior is about. Don't automatically assume that something went wrong with the visit. Discuss the problem with the other parent if you wish, but do so in a spirit of understanding. *Do not involve your child in this discussion.* Nor should you assume that your child's report of the visit is completely accurate. Remember that a young child will probably tell the custodial parent what she assumes that parent wants to hear. If you have given your child the strong message that you hate the very idea of her visiting the other parent, she will probably provide you with data to reinforce your point of view, even if she actually had a pretty good time.

One of the most serious visitation problems is the child's refusal to go. Eric was seven. After a custody dispute, he lived with his father and saw his mother every weekend and once during the week. Eventually, when his mother arrived to pick him up, Eric began clinging to his father's side, crying, "I don't want to go! I don't want to stay with Mommy! I want to stay with you!" On a few occasions he broke away from his father and started running down the street. Sometimes his mother would run after him and carry him to her car, while his father shouted back at her. Sometimes Eric's father would bring him back, saying to his ex-wife, "Look! Eric doesn't want to visit you today! Why don't you just forget about it?" Eric's mother always insisted on taking the child, all the while threatening her former husband with the loss of custody if he kept the child from her. Eric, of course, heard all this and would often cry.

His mother told a therapist called in to help that during the actual visits with her, Eric had a wonderful time. She was sure he was upset because he knew his father resented the visits. Dr. Lipton later had the opportunity of seeing Eric together with each parent. The child enjoyed being with his mother and when he was alone with the therapist, he refused to talk about why he ran away before the visits with her. Eric was able to say, however, that he definitely wanted the visits to continue. They did.

Sometimes a child's refusal to visit may have to do with some realistic fear of the other parent. Perhaps some actual abuse or neglect has taken place, or may even be ongoing. Usually, however, when children refuse visitation it is because their parents are acting out and interfering with the visitation. The custodial parent may cancel a scheduled visit with the other parent at the last minute or fail to be at home when that parent comes by to pick up the child. Sometimes the noncustodial parent will delay the child's return without informing the other parent in advance.

Such parental behavior is extremely destructive and harmful to the child. It interferes with the child's attempts to come to terms with the divorce and the custody decision, and is guaranteed to lead to psychological distress. Symptoms can range from bedwetting and sleep and eating disturbances in a younger child to withdrawal and depression or hostile and aggressive behavior in an older child.

And as if parental acting out were not bad enough, parents sometimes enlist others to play out their frustrations around visitation and other unresolved feelings after the custody dispute is over. It is not uncommon for such parents to call the police, for example, if they feel the other parent is sabotaging visits. If the child is late returning, the waiting parent may call the police to express the fear—real or imagined—that the child is being kidnapped. If a visiting parent comes to pick up the child and is denied access, he may call the police to resolve the issue. The police come, and the child witnesses an unpleasant and frightening scene. Police are often frustrated by these domestic disputes. They know that they rarely get a straight story from either parent, and that they can provide only a temporary solution to an ongoing domestic conflict.

Avoid involving the police in your visitation disputes unless you truly believe your child is in danger. You may think you've won the skirmish if the police come and take your side, but your child always loses. Nothing of substance will be resolved.

VISITATION PROBLEMS ARE bound to occur after a custody dispute. Scheduling conflicts, misunderstood messages, and distortions by parent and child alike can lead to trouble between even the most caring and concerned of parents. What can you do? First, review just what the problem is. When you're sure you know the answer, check with the other parent —not the child! Do not expect a child to provide an accurate report about the visitation. See if you and the other parent can work out an agreement, and try to give a little. The more reasonable you can be, the better the possibility of a resolution. Don't involve others in your dispute if you can help it. That goes for the police, family members, work associates, and neighbors. This is not the time to gather your forces against the other parent. Such action will be perceived as hostile and threatening and will only lead to further conflict.

If you and the other parent are not able to reach an agreement yourselves, then seek professional help before turning matters over to your lawyers. If you can, resist the urge to give up and turn to relitigation. Some short-term counseling with a neutral therapist may be enough to help both of you resolve the dispute. A qualified counselor can appeal to the best in each of you and to the love you both have for your child in assisting you to reach an understanding.

Unfortunately, troubled visitations can sometimes become chronic. April Repko was ten years old and lived with her mother. Her parents had been divorced since she was five. Her father, Harold Repko, had remarried. His new wife was a very successful businesswoman, the president of her own company. April lived with her mother, who had not remarried. After her successful custody fight, Ann Repko continued litigation concerning child support. Both parents were in and out of court for five years following the divorce. Whenever Ann was furious with her ex-husband, she would convince April to refuse to visit him. Whenever the child did see her father, her mother would telephone several times during the visit. This angered Harold, who saw these frequent calls as intrusive. To get back at his ex-wife, he frequently made appointments to pick up his daughter and then canceled them at the last minute. When he did visit, he would return April later than promised. Both parents did whatever they could to antagonize each other. At age ten, April developed psychogenic vomiting, that is, she would vomit when anxious. Once she had to be hospitalized for dehydration following a vomiting spell.

In cases like this, a teacher or pediatrician may suggest that a trusted therapist or counselor serve as an ongoing monitor. This person could meet with both parents on a regular basis and also see the child from time to time. Such advice should be heeded; it may represent the only glimmer of light in the long dark tunnel of chronic conflict.

Of course, situations may change as your child gets older. In general, some preteens and most teenagers will make their preferences regarding visitation very clear. They will follow their own visitation plan, one that fits into their schedule, regardless of your wishes, and it will become more and more difficult to impose your will on them. Parents should discuss visitation with their older children, but on the whole, they should allow them wide latitude in setting up a schedule.

Other factors, particularly remarriage, may bring changes in visitation. Sometimes a custodial parent who remarries would like to forget about the ex-spouse and finds the child's visits disruptive to the life of the new family. This parent might attempt to reduce the visits, claiming that the child has a whole family now and does not need as much contact with the noncustodial parent. The new spouse of a noncustodial parent may also resent the visits of a child from a previous marriage and view the child as an intruder. Divorced parents who remarry must be aware of their children's reaction and must not allow the new family to disrupt the children's easy and regular access to both of them.

Because of a remarriage, a better job, or both, a divorced parent may want to move away. Such a situation often pits a custodial parent's desire for a better life against the right of the child to have continuous, uninterrupted, easy access to the noncustodial parent. This particular issue often leads to relitigation as the noncustodial parent goes to court to stop the ex-spouse from moving away with the child. Judges have used the "best interests" presumption to guide them in these cases. In general, courts do not look favorably on granting custodial parents the right to move when such a move will seriously compromise the child's relationship with the noncustodial parent. A judge would have to be convinced that such a move was in the best interests of the child or that the child did not have a significant relationship with the noncustodial parent.

The best course in all visitation disputes is to be as flexible as you can, avoid more litigation if possible, and remain sensitive to the needs of your child. Remember that visitation is an opportunity for your child to continue a relationship forever changed by divorce and the custody dispute. It will be an important part of your child's life. There will always be times when you will want to wish it away. But the harder you try to make visitation work, the more your child will benefit.

RELITIGATION

EVEN AFTER A court decision, the custody dispute may not necessarily be over. It can be relitigated for years—sometimes until a child reaches adulthood. The only limiting factors for litigants who refuse to give up are money and determination. The more money a parent is prepared to spend and the more determined he or she is to secure custody, the longer a custody case can go on.

◻ PROS AND CONS ◻

There are legitimate as well as illegitimate reasons for relitigation. Most of those who decide to relitigate and thus to prolong the dispute do so because they believe it is in the child's best interests. A father may believe, for example, that the expert witness who advised the court to award custody to the mother was misinformed, prejudiced, or just plain incompetent. Or a mother may feel that her lawyer was lax, or that the judge was biased or inadequate. One parent may learn that the other has turned out to be an alcoholic and is endangering the safety of the children. Another parent previously treated for depression may become chronically depressed and refuse psychiatric help. Yet another may realize that the child has developed special needs that are not being met by the other parent.

In chapter 8 we examined the Emory custody case, in which Alice Emory was concerned that her husband's mental illness was damaging to Sara, their four-year-old daughter. Mr. Emory had been taking her to various emergency rooms and to private doctors, claiming that she was being harmed by her mother. During their custody trial, Mrs. Emory had claimed that her husband had a paranoid psychotic illness. He had countercharged that his wife was an alcoholic and herself a danger to the child. But the judge was not convinced that Mr. Emory was ill or that his behavior was detrimental to Sara's health, and chose to ignore the psychiatrist's recommendation.

Soon after the custody dispute had been decided in Mr. Emory's favor, Alice Emory entered an excellent substance-abuse rehabilitation center. She followed her stay there with regular attendance at Alcoholics Anonymous meetings; she had now been abstinent for over three years. Mr. Emory, meanwhile, had been hospitalized once with a documented psychotic episode.

Still concerned about Sara's visits with her father, Mrs. Emory reopened litigation. As part of that procedure, the family court judge appointed Dr. Bruce Feld to conduct a psychiatric evaluation of the family. At the joint session with Arthur Emory and Sara, Dr. Feld instructed them both simply to have fun together in the office and to play with whatever toys and games they wished. Dr. Feld was distressed at what he saw. Arthur Emory was watching Sara at the dollhouse as she played with a toy stove.

"Is that stove like the kind at Mommy's house?" Mr. Emory asked.

When Sarah answered yes, her father said, "Doesn't Mommy put your head in the oven sometimes and maybe even turn on the gas?"

"No!" Sara said immediately.

Mr. Emory pressed further. "Sara, didn't you once tell me that Mommy did that to punish you?"

"No," said Sara.

Dr. Feld remained silent and continued to observe Sara and her father. The child was now playing with the bathtub.

"Sara, why does Mommy put your head under the water when you take a bath?" Mr. Emory asked his daughter.

Sara did not answer and instead moved on to another toy.

"Sara, why does Mommy do that to you in the bathtub?" Mr. Emory persisted. When the child again refused to respond, her father turned to Dr. Feld and said, "She's afraid to tell the truth, because her mother might hurt her some more."

A few days later, Arthur Emory placed a late-night call to Dr. Feld's home. He told the physician that Sara had a scratch on her knee and that it had been caused by Alice scraping the child's skin with a sharp fork. With great anxiety, he told Dr. Feld that he was on his way to a local emergency room and was afraid that Sara might have to be admitted to the hospital with blood poisoning. According to the medical record reviewed later, the examining physician found no evidence of any scratch and sent the child home. Unfortunately, Mr. Emory contacted the child abuse hot line once again, and another complete investigation was initiated by child-abuse authorities.

After Dr. Feld recommended a change in the custody arrangement, the family court judge insisted that he testify to elaborate upon his written conclusions. During the cross-examination, Mr. Emory's lawyer attempted to discredit the doctor's diagnosis of Mr. Emory as having a paranoid disorder. The doctor agreed that, indeed, there was no evidence that Mr. Emory talked to himself, moved in a bizarre fashion, or showed indications of hallucinations. Still, said Dr. Feld, he believed Mr. Emory suffered from a psychotic illness.

"Dr. Feld, in plain English, is Mr. Emory mentally ill?" asked the judge rather bluntly.

"Yes, he is, your Honor," replied the physician.

"Do you see any hope of recovery?"

"Your Honor, Mr. Emory does not believe that he suffers from any mental illness and therefore has not sought treatment," said Dr. Feld. "This type of illness is usually chronic, unfortunately."

"What is the effect on the child, Doctor, of these trips to the emergency room and the child abuse investigations?"

Dr. Feld replied, "I think they're a form of child abuse themselves, and I'm afraid this sort of behavior will continue. The repeated physical examinations are unnecessary and psychologically harmful."

The judge reversed the original custody decision, and now gave Alice Emory sole custody. He also ordered that Mr. Emory have limited visitation with his daughter, and that these visits be supervised.

Although this relitigation was warranted and appropriate, not all relitigation is based on concern for the child. All too often, unfortunately, parents pursue relitigation out of vindictiveness: they cannot bear to see their ex-spouse "win," and relitigation becomes their way of taking revenge. One parent hopes that by filing motion after motion and forcing the other parent into court on a regular basis, that person will eventually "break" and admit defeat. The other parent is forced to use the adversarial system to fight back. In highly adversarial families, such cases may drag on for years. The result is an interminable custody dispute that can rob a child of his childhood and affect him throughout his life.

Betsy Smith lost custody of her seven-year-old son, Marc, to his father, Howard. During the custody trial, it had become apparent that Mr. Smith had always been Marc's primary caretaker. Mrs. Smith had admitted to several affairs which had led to frequent absences from home during Marc's early years. She, in turn, had accused her former husband of being an alcoholic. This had never been documented. During the psychiatric evaluation, Marc told the physician that he wanted to live with his father. After the decision, Marc visited his mother on alternate weekends and for one overnight during the week. He was doing well in school, had a number of friends and was coming to terms with his new life.

A year later, Mrs. Smith learned that the original judge had retired. She hired a new lawyer and a private detective, who photographed Mr. Smith having a drink in a bar. She and her lawyer then began new custody proceedings on the familiar grounds of alleged alcoholism. For the next year, the litigation proceeded until Mr. Smith's custody of Marc was reaffirmed. At this point, Marc was seeing a psychologist because of academic difficulties and problems in his relationships with other children. He was thought to have a moderate depression. Mrs. Smith was determined to press her demands and continued legal action for the next three years. She accused her former husband of obstructing the visitation, and this led to court hearings on two separate occasions. Finally, after her remarriage, she stopped litigating.

□ THE TRAUMA OF □
RELITIGATION

Little research exists about the effects of relitigating custody or visitation upon the child, a fact that probably reflects the overall tendency of researchers to focus on parental behavior rather than upon the child's experience. But reviewing the psychological effects of a custody dispute in general will give you some idea of the impact of continued litigation upon a child. A young child feels distressed, frightened, and confused by what is happening. He may cry frequently, develop fears, or manifest physical symptoms such as bed-wetting, vomiting, diarrhea, or rashes. Older children can become depressed and angry and display behavioral symptoms such as aggression, stealing, or self-destructive patterns.

When parents engage in constant, unremitting litigation, there is never any peace in the home. The child is constantly caught in the middle of the parents' battle and regularly forced to choose sides. As judges reverse or modify custody or visitation arrangements, the child's already fragile routine is repeatedly disrupted. Nothing is certain—except that the conflict will continue. If there is an ongoing dispute over visitation, every visit becomes a tension packed experience. The police may even be called, an event that intensifies the child's constant fear of losing the relationship with one or the other parent at any time. In drawn-out litigations, various judges may see the child *in camera*. Even if a judge is gentle and understanding, these repeated interviews can put added stress upon the child. It is therefore fair to say that a child subjected to chronic custody litigation is emotionally burdened almost beyond endurance.

And what of the parents? For some, the legal case becomes all-consuming. Lawyers are hired, then fired. An endless parade of new witnesses and other experts keeps the case alive. In pursuit of custody, parents may also move to another state or try to change courts. For such parents, even those who take pleasure in the constant struggle, there is no such thing as a normal home life. A tremendous amount of psychic and physical energy is taken up with the legal proceedings, and the relitigation becomes a crusade with its own set of exclusive truths. Litigious parents see themselves as the only ones who know how dangerous it is for the child to be with the custodial parent, who is perceived as evil, a monster, a liar, and often a psychopath. Anyone not on the "right" side becomes the enemy.

Since a custody dispute most frequently forms the basis for relitigation, the question of joint custody arises. Does a joint custody arrangement offer any protection against relitigation? Unfortunately, data here are inconclusive. California psychiatrist Frederic W. Ilfeld and his research team studied 414 consecutive custody cases before a Los Angeles court over a two-year period and found that joint custody families had 50 percent fewer incidences of relitigation than sole custody families.[1] Their conclusion was that the custody arrangement most conducive to no further parental relitigation was joint custody. However, they also found that relitigation rates were high when joint custody was imposed by the court.

Other studies, however, have suggested that the incidence of relitigation following a custody trial is just as high with joint custody as with sole custody. Drs. Peter Ash and Melvin Guyer, researchers at the University of Michigan School of Medicine, dispute the conclusions of Ilfeld and his team. They followed 104 families originally referred to their clinic for custody evaluations.[2] Their study concluded that joint custody arrangements did not automatically offer any protection against relitigation. In fact, there may be no direct relationship between parental dissatisfaction and the decision to relitigate, nor is there any evidence that relitigation is related to any particular custody arrangement. It may also be a mistake to assume that the absence of relitigation means that a custody arrangement is working well for a family. The personality characteristics and financial resources of the parents may be the real determining factors.

□ **TOUGH CHOICES** □

It should be repeated that not all parents who choose to relitigate are emotionally disturbed or thirsting for revenge. Some genuinely believe that their child would be better off with them, or that the court should reconsider the visitation arrangements—especially when a parent feels that visitation is being obstructed. Some parents have good reason to keep their custody case open.

On the positive side, relitigation can provide a mechanism for protecting the best interests of the child if circumstances change. A change in the custodial parent's situation, such as the onset of an illness that directly affects the ability to care for the child; the parent's involvement with anyone whose behavior is detrimental to the child's welfare; constant obstruction of the child's visitation with the noncustodial parent; or a unilateral plan to move far from the noncustodial parent—all these are good reasons for relitigation. The noncustodial parent can alert the court that new criteria for "best interests" need to be applied; the court may be convinced that unforeseen circumstances necessitate further judicial involvement. Thus, theoretically at least, the possibility of relitigation can serve to monitor the child's needs and the family situation. In addition, its availability offers noncustodial parents another day in court to present their case—a desirable option if the first custody arrangement has been found deficient or dangerous, or if new evidence that might influence a custody or visitation decision has been uncovered.

Paradoxically, the possibility of relitigation may encourage adversaries to work out some sort of mediated settlement. The specter of years and years of court proceedings can motivate the parties to seek an out-of-court settlement. To avoid litigation, they may choose to work with a therapist to reach agreement on disputed issues. After an experience with litigation, reasonable parents may realize the cost to them and their children of repeated court appearances and be more inclined to seek agreement.

Still, the disadvantages of relitigation cannot be reviewed too often. Relitigation prolongs the agony of the divorce and the custody dispute. As long as it continues, neither parents nor children are able to work through the pain and suffering of the breakup of the family; instead, they experience chronic stress and the psychological trauma that comes with unremitting conflict. Usually the child, who has only limited resources with which to cope with this pressure, suffers the most.

Second, relitigation can represent a gross misuse of the adversarial system by those fortunate enough to have money. Motivated by vindictiveness or even sadism, a wealthy parent may return to court repeatedly, hoping to inflict pain upon the other parent or sometimes even upon the child. Such a parent may claim to have the child's best interests at heart, but this is often not the case at all.

What should you do about relitigation and the monumental problems it brings? The best answer is to do all you can to prevent it from occurring at all. As with every other aspect of custody discussed in this book, making your child the focus of your concerns will point you in the right direction.

Seek out a child behavior expert to gain some objective insight about the potential effect upon your child of more legal proceedings. Consider other alternatives, such as mediation or arbitration by a psychiatrist or psychologist. No matter how unfairly you feel you have been treated, think of relitigation as a last resort, when every other avenue has proved unsuccessful.

If, however, you see it as the only alternative, make sure you and your lawyer keep the focus on your child rather than on victory over the other parent. Ongoing relitigation becomes a true nightmare for the family and is guaranteed to cause immeasurable pain to all. Children need time and an end to conflict in order to begin recovering. So do you.

DOES YOUR CHILD
NEED THERAPY?

A CUSTODY DISPUTE subjects parents and children to chronic stress. There have probably been days when you felt you could not endure another minute of conflict, and you know your child feels the same. Even if the litigation is over, you are probably still worried about how well your child has survived the fight. Because virtually all children experience some psychological symptoms during divorce and custody disputes, you need to be especially aware of the kinds of symptoms your child might display. You need to know when symptoms are severe enough to warrant professional intervention. Don't wait until your child seems out of control or in the middle of a psychiatric emergency before you seek help. Symptoms requiring such help may at first seem mild—such as sleep disturbances or anxiety—or only moderate—such as frequent anger or academic problems. Don't let these escalate into profound withdrawal or depression.

When his father moved out of the house and he became aware of his parents' custody battle, Jason, six years old, developed problems. Although both parents tried to shield Jason from their mutual antagonism, he was an extremely sensitive child and easily picked up on the family tensions. He began to have trouble falling asleep and would demand that his mother stay in bed with him; sometimes he came into her room in the middle of the night. His mother felt uncomfortable about having him in her bed, but she also felt guilty about returning him, crying, to his own room. Jason's father said his son behaved in the same way when he was with him. Jason also suffered frequent nightmares, and once he had a night terror. (A night terror is a disturbance in which a child wakes suddenly from a deep sleep and, apparently terrified, begins to scream and cry, perhaps sweating and showing a rapid pulse as well. After a few minutes, the child calms down and falls back to sleep, without ever having fully awakened. There is usually no memory of the episode in the morning. Although night terrors are frightening for parents to witness, they are not usually dangerous for the child.)

Jason's separation anxiety was also marked by his crying and hanging on whenever he had to leave one of his parents. Often, he would cry and even vomit when his father or mother went out for the evening and left him with a babysitter. Although he had initially done very well when he went to kindergarten, he was now having trouble going to school in the morning. And he was frequently in the nurse's office, complaining of a "bellyache" and insisting on going home.

Kira was ten when her parents began their divorce proceedings and custody dispute. They had been in a mediation program that failed, and their relationship was now quite hostile. Whenever Kira traveled between her father's city apartment and her mother's suburban home, she would cry. She found it hard to leave either parent. Her schoolwork suffered too; she couldn't concentrate on her homework or on studying for tests, which she'd always been proud of doing. She started talking back to her teacher—something she had never done before. At home, Kira was alternately outspoken and angry or sullen and withdrawn—typical signs of an adjustment disorder. When she saw her mother crying or heard her shouting at her father over the telephone, she would scream, "I can't stand this!" and run into her room, slamming the door.

Matthew, twelve, lived with his father following a custody dispute. The litigation had lasted more than four years, draining both parents' financial and emotional resources. As well as winning the custody dispute, Matthew's father also won the right to move to another state, reducing the child's access to his mother.

About three months after he and his father had moved, Matthew developed symptoms of a severe depression. He became withdrawn; he lost his appetite. He had trouble falling asleep and would wake up many times during the night. He complained of all sorts of physical ailments. He refused to bathe himself or brush his teeth. He cried a lot and talked about not wanting to live any longer. His father's friends reassured the father that these feelings were normal after such a major move, but when Matthew's grief persisted for two more months, his father became alarmed and took him to a pediatrician. After an emergency consultation with a child psychiatrist, Matthew was admitted to a psychiatric ward in a nearby hospital.

In these cases, all three children needed psychiatric help, although only Matthew was affected severely enough to require hospitalization. Jason and Kira were treated on an outpatient basis by a mental health professional.

□ WHEN TO SEEK HELP □

Since it is common for children to develop symptoms of psychological distress during divorce and custody disputes, how can you tell whether your own child needs professional help?

The first thing to do is simply to observe your child. You know him and his routines better than anyone. Watch how he goes about his daily activities. Your four-year-old, for example, does he seem the same as he did before your family problems began? If he goes to nursery school or to a day care center, how does he behave when you separate? At home, does he play with other children in the same way as before? Is he more aggressive, or more withdrawn? Can he share with other children? Does he get into more arguments? Are his eating and sleeping habits the same? Has his appetite changed? Has he developed any sleep disturbances, such as bed-wetting, nightmares, night terrors, or sleepwalking? Does he complain of physical problems such as abdominal pain, an upset stomach, or headaches? You can also check with your child's nursery school teacher, day care leader, or babysitters to learn whether there has been any significant change in his behavior.

For a seven- or eight-year-old, two major areas of functioning are crucial to development: schoolwork and peer relations. You should assess both to learn whether your child is having problems. How is she handling school? Is she able to concentrate on homework? Can she study effectively for tests? Do teachers report any changes in her behavior? How does she relate to her friends and other children her own age? Do you notice any changes, such as a decline in interest in social activities, or more arguments with other children? What about changes in basic daily routines, such as eating, sleeping, and personal hygiene?

Older children—preteens and teenagers—are often occupied with a busy social life. This usually includes membership in after-school clubs or team sports, going to dances or parties, and dating. Observe how your child participates in these activities, and look for changes in routines. Remember that a child's reaction to stress and anxiety will often be to act out or act in. An older child's acting in includes withdrawing and spending more time alone, cutting down on contact with peers—either over the telephone or in person—and complaining about physical problems. Acting out is reflected in a change in the quality of behavior: a new group of friends or a shift of interest from sports and clubs to risks and trouble such as drug use or vandalism. The child might become a truant, or develop behavior problems at school.

Talk to your child. Find out how she feels about the custody dispute. Many parents in a dispute do everything *except* discuss it with their children. Like Matthew's father, most parents want to deny that the dispute is harming the child, and prefer to act as if everything at home is just the same. The ostrich approach may work, but not for long. Some parents also feel that they are protecting their child if they avoid discussing the custody battle. Sometimes one parent will discuss it with the child, but the other will not. The child then becomes even more confused, while "to talk" or "not to talk" becomes yet another bone of contention between the parents. It is common for court-appointed experts evaluating custody disputes to hear from one parent that the other has explained too much to the child; the "explaining" parent will maintain that the other keeps the child in the dark.

When you do talk to your child, you can learn more about how he is handling the custody dispute. Some children are more open than others. Be prepared for a variety of reactions, from extreme anger to complete denial of any distress. Whatever your child's reaction, you will have gained information that can help you decide whether or not to seek professional help. You can start your talk very generally. Do you know what's going on? What Mom and Dad are arguing about? What's it like for you when we fight? Some kids get scared when they hear about judges and lawyers and courtrooms—do you? Do you worry about all this at school? When you do your homework? At night? Do you know any other kids who have gone through a custody dispute? How are they dealing with it? What can I do to make it better or easier for you?

A child needs professional help if he or she seems regularly unhappy or anxious. The key here is "regularly," meaning that the problem is a chronic one. Basically, such a child will not be functioning normally in day-to-day activities. Relationships with other children might be impaired. The child may be overly aggressive, unable to share, or withdrawn. He may not be able to separate from the parent. There may be more physical symptoms, such as abdominal pain, headaches, hives, appetite problems, and sleep disturbances. If the child is older, he may not be able to concentrate in school, and grades may be affected.

Before, during, or after a custody dispute, it is always a good idea to consult with a mental health professional who has some expertise in this area. Such a person can help you gain insight into what children go through emotionally during a custody dispute, and how you can be more sensitive to their needs. A therapist can also evaluate whether or not your child shows signs of chronic anxiety and might benefit from professional counseling. (Before you ask for a consultation, be clear in your own mind that you are seeking this professional's help in a *therapeutic* context, and that you have no intention of involving the person in any litigation. An experienced clinician will clarify this with you anyway.)

The therapist usually spends several sessions with the child in order to make the evaluation, and will want to meet with the parents as well. He may also contact teachers or other important people in the child's life. From all these observations, he develops an opinion about the child's symptoms and recommends a plan for treatment. If the parents are also meeting with the therapist on a regular basis, the case may require only a few months' treatment. However, some children may require therapy for several years.

In the best of all worlds, it would make sense for you and the other parent to consult the same person, either separately or in a joint session; that way, the clinician can get a better sense of the impact your dispute is having on your child. In some custody disputes, however, there is so much hostility between the parents that they cannot bear to be in the same room. In such a case, it would be unlikely that they would agree to sit together in a therapist's office.

Harry Stern and his wife were in a custody battle over their seven-year-old daughter, Lucy. Mr. Stern, ironically a divorce lawyer himself, called Dr. Bethel, a child psychologist, to arrange a consultation for himself. He was concerned about the effects of the custody dispute on his daughter. In particular, he was worried because he and his wife still lived in the same house, and he feared that the constant domestic tension was detrimental to their child. Dr. Bethel asked whether Mrs. Stern would be coming along. "I doubt it," Mr. Stern said. "She would reject anyone I suggested just on principle. She hardly talks to me as it is."

Dr. Bethel nonetheless suggested that Mr. Stern invite his wife to participate. He did, but she refused. Dr. Bethel then agreed to see Mr. Stern alone. During the session, Mr. Stern reported that his wife had initiated divorce proceedings one year before, and that they had been unable to come to an out-of-court settlement on the custody of Lucy.

Mr. Stern acknowledged the irony of being the client in a custody matter. He said he always had known it was stressful for both parents and children, but he never had dreamed it would be as difficult as it was. On advice of counsel, he said, he had remained in the family home, but it was becoming an untenable situation for everyone. The week before, his daughter had broken down and had been unable to stop crying. He finally saw clearly, he said, just how much she was being hurt by the dispute.

Dr. Bethel encouraged Mr. Stern to work out some other living arrangement. He also told Mr. Stern that although he believed Lucy needed therapeutic intervention, it would not be a good idea to bring her to see him against her mother's wishes. This would only aggravate a difficult situation. Instead, Dr. Bethel suggested that Mr. Stern ask his wife to seek a therapeutic consultation for their child and that he go along with what-ever arrangement she made. He urged Mr. Stern to do his utmost to separate the issue of an evaluation and possible psychological treatment of the child from the custody conflict.

At first, Mr. Stern objected. Why should he have to go along with his wife's wishes in this matter when she wouldn't do the same for him? In fact, he told Dr. Bethel that he and his lawyer had discussed filing a motion to force his wife to agree to therapy for Lucy on the grounds that the child was being emotionally harmed every day and that her mother seemed to have an utter lack of regard for her welfare. Dr. Bethel acknowledged that Mr. Stern must be furious with his wife for this and many other reasons. He suggested, though, that Mr. Stern do what he could to put aside his anger on this particular issue. He urged Mr. Stern to press his wife to seek professional help for Lucy and to cooperate with her as much as he could. Dr. Bethel pointed out that if Lucy were taken from one therapist to another because the parents could not agree on a single individual, she would become even more upset, confused, and frustrated.

In this case, Mr. Stern may have forestalled further anxiety for his child. Dr. Bethel was able to make a therapeutic intervention without becoming directly involved with the child. He shared with Mr. Stern an important concept, which you need to remember as well: *Do not allow your child to be taken from one therapist to another because you and the other parent cannot agree on one person.* Unless your child is in the middle of a true crisis, it is better to put off contact with a therapist until the issue can be resolved. If, however, he has a psychotic episode, or exhibits behavior that indicates the presence of suicidal thoughts—such as deliberately hurting himself, having an unusual number of "accidents," being careless in traffic, or engaging in risk-taking—then it is time to take action. But avoid "therapist shopping"; many of the legal professionals involved in custody cases are not always aware of the potential harm to the child of seeing multiple therapists during this period.

Judge Maxwell Albert thought that he had the child's best interests in mind during the Lorbers' dispute over the custody of their eight-year-old son, Will. Will was in the third grade and was having problems getting along with other children and completing school assignments. One by one, his friends had stopped playing with him because of his increasing aggressiveness. This aggravated his misbehavior, and Will became increasingly more sullen and resentful. The Lorbers decided that he should see a therapist, but they were unable to agree on the same individual. As a result, Will was taken to several child therapists for relatively brief evaluations.

When Mrs. Lorber's lawyer objected to Judge Albert that Will was seeing too many therapists, the judge issued an order in response. But instead of addressing the problem of Will's going to several therapists, the judge's order stated:

> Each parent agrees to consult with the other as to any psychological services they are requesting for Will Lorber, their son. They will exchange any and all reports coming out of these services. Alan and Sherry Lorber are each permitted to obtain whatever psychological services they deem necessary for their son. Any of these individual psychological services may communicate with the other.

Unfortunately, this court order actually gave the Lorbers permission to choose whichever therapist each of them wanted, and to change therapists if they so desired. The order stated that they had to "consult" with each another, not "agree" with each other. The Lorbers decided that "consult" simply meant "inform," and that is what they did. Will was seen by four different therapists over a two-month period. When he was evaluated (yet again!) by the court-appointed child psychiatrist, Will expressed his anger at having to see so many different "shrinks." He said he liked one that his father had picked out and was then confused and angry when his mother took him to another one. The third one, another of his father's choices, did not rate highly with the child. Will told the evaluating psychiatrist: "All my parents do is fight with each other. They say they want to help me, but I don't believe them. They're the ones who should be seeing a psychiatrist—not me!"

□ PREPARING FOR THERAPY □

Let's assume a positive scenario in which you and the other parent have agreed that your child should see a mental health professional. If you have already been awarded sole custody of your child, this is a decision you can make on your own. However, it would still be in your child's best interests to involve the noncustodial parent in this process from the start. And if you are in a joint custody situation, you and the other parent probably have—or should have—an implicit bargain to agree on such an important move.

You will have a wide range of practitioners to choose from: psychiatrists, psychologists, psychiatric social workers. Bear in mind too that psychotherapy is not just for the rich, and that psychological evaluation and treatment are available to everyone in the United States, whatever their ability to pay. Private practitioners' fees can range from about $45 per session, charged by a psychiatric social worker, to more than $150 per session, charged by a psychiatrist. If you cannot afford these fees, however, you do have other alternatives. Every community in the country is divided into mental health catchment areas with access to specific mental health centers. The centers may be community agencies or clinics within hospitals or larger medical centers. You can call the psychiatry department of your local hospital to learn about your catchment area and its mental health center. Some communities also have mental health and counseling centers that are private but still offer lower fees. This may be because they have special endowments or serve as training sites for education and research. Although you may be assigned someone still in training as a mental health professional, you and your child can still receive superb treatment.

Younger people in this field are often extremely dedicated and have a great deal of energy. They will be supervised by an experienced therapist, and you and your family will have the added benefit of the supervisor's expertise.

You can find out about local clinics and mental health professionals in your area by calling any of the following: the psychiatry department of a nearby medical school, the state, district or local branch of the American Psychiatric Association, or the Washington, D.C. offices of the American Academy of Child and Adolescent Psychiatry (see Appendix). This association will be able to refer you to child psychiatrists in your area, including those who specialize in divorce and custody issues. A child psychiatrist in your area can help you find a suitable professional for your family if his own fee is too high for you, or if your insurance coverage is inadequate. A school counselor may be able to recommend a therapist. And don't be afraid to ask therapists if they have some flexibility in setting the fee. Many do.

When you do choose a therapist for your child, she may ask to see you and the other parent together. If you can set aside your differences long enough to meet with her, you should. A joint meeting will allow her not only to learn both sides of your story, but also to see how you act toward each other and gain a sense of what your child may be experiencing in interacting with you.

A child psychiatrist was treating an eight-year-old girl whose parents were locked in a major dispute over visitation. The mother was the sole custodial parent, but the father had threatened that if the dispute was not settled soon, he would begin new litigation to gain sole custody. The therapist met with both parents and realized that they had never truly divorced themselves emotionally from each other. They were coy and almost flirtatious with each other, yet this flirtation could quickly turn to fury. The therapist could see how the parents' behavior must have confused their child and played into her fantasies about their becoming reconciled.

. . .

AT THE FIRST meeting, tell the therapist all your concerns about your child. You can review what you have observed in the child's behavior and relay the gist of important conversations you have had together. You might want to mention schoolwork and what teachers have reported to you. The therapist will want to know about your child's history and development, experiences, likes and dislikes, as well as something about your own life and childhood. All this background material will help her get a detailed picture of your child's world and the effect of the family breakup on it.

When the time comes for the child to have an individual session, the therapist will help you to prepare him. Be honest with your child about the visit. If the child is three or four years old, you can say something like this: "The family has been through a lot lately, and we've all been upset. We're going to take you to a special doctor who is just going to talk to you to see how you are and to help us all feel a little better." Sometimes parents don't like to use the word "doctor" in this context, for they feel it will make their child anxious. They use euphemisms like "a nice man," or "a lady who plays with children" instead of saying "Dr. Smith." This only confuses a young child and certainly does not fool an older one. The more comfortable you yourself can be about seeing the therapist, the easier it will be for your child. You can say, "Dr. Smith is a talking doctor for kids. She likes to talk and sometimes plays games with kids and helps them with their worries and fears. I've already met her and she's very nice. I think she can help us all feel better."

A child of five or six can be told about the session a day or so before the appointment. An older child should have a few days' notice to talk about it with you and to feel that she has time to plan for it. Offer your child the opportunity to talk about the appointment, but don't insist that she tell you how she feels. Usually, a younger child will not object to going; a child of nine or ten might. Children of this age begin to feel that going to a psychiatrist or psychologist means someone thinks they are "crazy." They are also worried about other children finding out. You can tell your child that no one thinks they are "sick," and that therapists work with lots of different kinds of kids. Furthermore, you are not asking for a commitment to regular therapy—just to meet the therapist for a few sessions. Most children will agree to this.

Avoid the tendency to suggest the agenda for a session with your child. For example, she might indicate that something is troubling her or you, or you might have just quarreled. You may be inclined to say, "Why don't you bring this up with Dr. Green? See what he thinks." This kind of suggestion, while well intentioned, intrudes on the child's special relationship with the therapist. Allow your child to set her own agenda. Therapists know that children eventually bring up the important issues in their own way. It will have far more meaning for your child to be able to do that when she is ready. If there is something you feel the therapist must know prior to your child's session, you can always call. But keep such calls to a minimum. Allow your child the space and time to reveal herself comfortably to the therapist. It will make the experience a much more positive one.

After the first session is over, resist the temptation to question your child about how things went. Don't ask what she and the therapist talked about, how she felt being there, whether she liked the person, and so on. Allow her to absorb this experience in her own way and on her own schedule. She may or may not wish to discuss it with you. She has a right to her privacy in this situation, just as you do.

What actually goes on between your child and this professional behind that closed door? How can the therapist help a child who has gone through a custody battle? Why do therapists play games with children? What can they learn from them? Will your child really talk about what is bothering her? What is the therapist looking for?

A therapist may be impressed by separation anxiety if the child cannot tolerate being alone in the office without a parent.

He watches the child's movements for signs of hyperactivity, listens to her voice for signs of anxiety or fearfulness and looks for other signs, such as nail-biting and tics, or for indications of self-abuse, such as head-banging. He listens for warning signals that the child is unhappy or has very low self-esteem. Gradually, the therapist works to develop a warm, nurturing relationship with the child.

The therapist's major goal, in fact, is to develop this easy working relationship. It may take a number of sessions before the child feels comfortable enough to begin to trust. If she has been able to trust you in the past, and if you express your approval of and confidence in the therapist, your child has an excellent chance of developing a good relationship with him. Child therapists know they must proceed slowly in order to give the child a chance to feel at ease. You may find yourself impatient and want things to "feel better" a bit faster than is really possible.

After the divorce and custody dispute, Diane Patterson, who now had sole custody of Michael, age nine, brought her son to Dr. Hewitt for therapy. During the last year, Michael had become very sullen and angry. His grades had dropped and his friendships decreased. In addition, he had been having episodes of bizarre and destructive behavior, which he could not explain; he had cut up a pair of his mother's gloves and had then denied that he had done so. On another occasion, he had thrown water balloons out of the window of his room, hitting passersby. He offered no explanation for these acts, and would burst into uncontrollable crying when he was asked about them.

Diane Patterson had been in therapy herself and was very hopeful that Dr. Hewitt could help her son. Although Michael's father, Richard, agreed that his son should see a therapist, he was extremely wary. Before Michael's visit, he met alone with Dr. Hewitt and told the psychologist that he had very little faith in therapy.

"His mother has been going for seven years," said Mr. Patterson, "and it hasn't done her a damn bit of good. In fact, I think it was her therapist who convinced her to get the divorce in the first place. Anyway, there's not that much wrong with Michael that I can see. I did the same sort of thing when I was a kid. Boys do that."

Later in the session, Mr. Patterson said: "You ought to know, Dr. Hewitt, that if Michael doesn't want to come here, he won't. He's very stubborn sometimes. His mother took him to some therapist two years ago, and he never went back. He said the woman was a jerk and asked him stupid questions."

Dr. Hewitt expressed the hope that Michael would come in, and that Mr. Patterson would give the evaluation and therapy a chance to work. The therapist knew that Mr. Patterson's disapproval could easily influence the child. From Mr. Patterson's manner, Dr. Hewitt also assumed Michael's father might be looking for a confrontation and a way to express his anger. The therapist knew that it was another child psychologist, appointed by the court, who had recommended that Mrs. Patterson have sole custody. Dr. Hewitt wisely avoided any encounter that could be construed as adversarial by Michael's father. His hope was to be able to gain his confidence, or at least his neutrality, so that Michael himself could give the therapeutic process a chance without being burdened by his father's strong resistance to his visits.

Dr. Hewitt moved very slowly with Michael. He understood that the boy was angry at being there and was extremely reluctant to speak. Michael sat on the couch in a very stiff posture, saying nothing except in response to questions. Dr. Hewitt did the talking. He told Michael that although he could not feel what the child had gone through, he could imagine a few things. He said that he knew kids who go through divorce and custody disputes have all kinds of mixed-up feelings and that many of them are angry but are afraid to show it. He told Michael he would never tell a parent to force a child to see him, because he knew that could never help. He expressed the hope that he and Michael could get to know each other over time and that maybe he would be able to help the boy sort out his feelings. Michael remained quiet. Then Dr. Hewitt, pointing to a selection on a nearby shelf, asked him if he wanted to play a game. Michael smiled, picked up a deck of cards, and said, "Let's play war!" The therapy had begun.

IN A TRUSTING therapeutic relationship, the therapist helps the child feel free to express the many feelings he is experiencing. The therapist gives the child permission to be himself in the office, to say anything on his mind, to speak or be silent, to be angry or happy.

Therapists know that children who have experienced custody disputes still have confused loyalties and all kinds of contradictory feelings about both parents. The therapist helps the child understand these loyalties and guides the healing process. The therapist also works to improve the child's self-esteem, which may have been damaged.

Older children often can talk directly about what has been bothering them, but younger ones may find it easier to communicate through play. The therapist does indeed play games with the child, including checkers, cards, board games like Candyland, Sorry!, or Chutes and Ladders, or fantasy games made up by the child. The two may also draw or paint together, or build something out of blocks. But there is more to this process than just play. The therapist observes how the child plays, whether he cheats or follows rules, the child's level of frustration, whether he can win comfortably or lose graciously, the content of the fantasy play, and so on. All this information helps the therapist understand the child's psychological world, how he feels about himself, and how he goes about maintaining his relationships with others.

Some children, for example, cannot tolerate losing. They will cheat to avoid it, then deny vehemently that they are doing so. They feel at a disadvantage in the world and use whatever tricks they can to "make it." Others are afraid of beating the therapist at a game, and so they will "help" him to win. These children often fear antagonizing an adult and thus risking the loss of emotional security. The therapist can learn much from the play and can then at appropriate times interpret for the child what his behavior is suggesting. Here are some examples.

An eleven-year-old boy purposely allowed the therapist to beat him repeatedly at checkers. He was smart enough to play a better game, but he told the doctor: "A little boy shouldn't beat a grown-up. It's okay; I don't mind losing." Later in his therapy, he told the doctor that he was always afraid his father would be angry with him for not obeying all the rules at home. He also thought that if he was good, maybe his parents would be so happy with him that they could be happy with each other again.

A five-year-old girl whose parents were divorcing was playing at the dollhouse in her psychiatrist's office. She took some little dolls and pushed them out of the window over and over again. She arranged for another doll to fall off the roof. The mother and father dolls fell down the stairs. During this time, the child was agitated and fearful. She said to the therapist, "Everyone is falling out of the house. No one will be left. It's a big mess." The therapist said to her, "Sometimes, when a mommy and a daddy don't live with each other any more, the whole house falls apart. It's a big mess, too." The child said, "Right." Then she said, "Let's draw a picture of my house when I grow up. It's gonna be a nice one." The therapist had made an interpretation to the child. That is, she had related the child's play to what she was experiencing emotionally. This helps a child understand her feelings and begin the healing process.

Besides this traditional form of one-on-one therapy, there is another option for your child: group therapy. Children who have particular problems in relating to others or who need to develop social skills can sometimes benefit from group treatment. Certain specialized groups—children whose parents have divorced or children whose parents have engaged in custody disputes—can offer young people an opportunity to discuss very personal issues in an understanding and supportive atmosphere.

Some schools now offer such groups for students who have experienced or are going through a family breakup. They may be led by teachers, guidance counselors, or psychiatric social workers. One such program in use nationwide is called Banana Splits (see Appendix). It was developed more than a decade ago by a social worker who recognized that school-age children need help after divorce. The program has been used for children of all ages and—depending upon the child's age and situation —involves group activities as well as talk sessions. Children who attend know that what they talk about will be treated as confidential, and that they are not alone with their complex feelings.

If your child's school has such a program, find out who runs it and what their credentials are. Find parents whose children have participated and who might be willing to talk with you. This program could be beneficial to your child; just be sure that you investigate it carefully and responsibly, as you would an individual therapist for your child.

With the therapist as a facilitator, and with normal development serving as the friendly, unseen ally of the therapist, your child can recover from the conflict and go on to lead a happier life.

CONCLUSION: IS THERE LIFE AFTER A CUSTODY DISPUTE?

RESUMING NORMAL LIFE after a custody dispute may seem like an impossible dream. For so long, life has been an endless series of crises, of major and minor tragedies. You have seen your marriage dissolve and your family break apart in a way you never thought possible. Perhaps most painful, you have seen your child suffer and have been unable to take away the hurt. You have worried about your son or daughter every step of the way. Perhaps you have consulted a therapist to help your child and perhaps you are in therapy yourself. If so, you probably are able to monitor your moods well enough to know that both you and your child have good days and bad days. If you are the parent who has been granted custody, you will naturally feel more optimistic about the future than if you have suffered a defeat. But regardless of your legal status, you will often wonder just what kind of life there is after a custody dispute.

As we've seen, the trauma of divorce can be long-lasting. Everyone suffers and grieves long after the litigation is over. Parents continue to feel guilt over the family breakup, even if they realize it was for the best and that they could never have stayed together "for the sake of the children." And the conflict and animosity of a custody dispute—especially one in which litigation is prolonged—is sure to leave even deeper scars. Before parents are able to work through their feelings of loss and disappointment at the marital breakup, they have turned into adversaries. Before children are able to begin to assimilate the meaning of the divorce and to begin to accommodate to it, they have become pawns in the hands of litigating parents. But as we have observed repeatedly, most children are simply unable to muster enough mature defense mechanisms to come through all of this unscathed. So no matter what pain you yourself may be experiencing, it is your responsibility to protect your child from the most damaging consequences of this traumatic period.

The greatest fear of a very young child is abandonment. Even without fully comprehending the meaning of a custody dispute, a young child fears being left alone, and the fear might be compounded if one parent says that this in fact might happen. As you know, in the midst of a custody dispute, parents often say terrible things to children about the other parent. Even a seemingly mild statement, like "Daddy won't be seeing you for a little while," might be perceived by the child as a prelude to abandonment. Whether the child's worst fears are actually confirmed or not, fear or abandonment may remain throughout childhood.

Children of four to six or seven often feel that they are the cause of divorce. Their own guilt, born out of their developmentally appropriate egocentrism, can be exaggerated when they see their parents locked in what appears to be mortal combat. It can be terrifying for children to see their parents fight with each other, even if the battle is purely verbal. And even after the battle ends, chronic anxiety can persist.

For example, three years after his parents' custody battle, Gary Nelson, now six years old, still had several symptoms of anxiety. He had begun to bite his nails, and although he had been completely toilet-trained at age two, when the custody fight began, Gary reverted to wetting his pants during the day and wetting his bed at night. He lived with his mother and visited his father intermittently, but neither scolding nor cajoling and rewarding by either of his parents could stop the enuresis. Gary would sometimes have several "dry" weeks, but during and after every visit with his father, he would wet his pants again. Gary's parents were appalled at his behavior and punished him by taking away television privileges and his favorite foods, which of course only made him feel worse. What they did not realize was that Gary's behavior was not malicious, but a sign of his continuing distress.

For some children, and their parents, life *after* a custody dispute can be almost as upsetting as it was during the litigation. So much depends on how parents handle themselves. Ned and Sarah Brodlie had been engaged in a custody dispute for three years. When their son, Edward, was seven years old, custody was awarded to Sarah. During the litigation, Sarah had accused her husband of sexually abusing the boy. An investigation determined the charges to be unfounded. However, Sarah continued to believe that Ned was abusing her son. For years after the dispute was settled, Ned and Sarah were in court, arguing mostly over visitation. Sarah would charge that her ex-husband was molesting the boy; he would accuse her of being a paranoid schizophrenic and of brainwashing Edward. Each hired and fired lawyers regularly.

Edward, in the first grade, was doing poorly in school. He had been placed in a special education class for emotionally disturbed children. He seemed too distracted to learn. He was refusing to read. He hit other children and had temper tantrums in the middle of class. He would curse at his teacher. His temper tantrums at home became violent. He broke things in his mother's home and kicked her. At other times, he would simply withdraw to his room and cry incessantly.

Sarah took her son to a therapist. He asked to see Mr. Brodlie, but Edward's mother lied to the therapist and said that Ned was not interested in seeing him. Naïvely believing Mrs. Brodlie, Dr. Grant treated the boy for six months. When Mr. Brodlie found out what was happening, he was furious. He threatened to sue Dr. Grant for malpractice, and went to court to move for the cessation of the therapy and for a change in custody. The judge did not grant the custody change but did order therapy to stop, pending an evaluation of Dr. Grant's treatment by a court-appointed therapist. Therapy was halted for three months, and Edwards' symptoms became worse. The battle between Edward's parents continued throughout his childhood and despite reentering therapy, Edward had chronic problems making and keeping friends, doing his schoolwork, and improving his self-esteem. He became a bully.

As we have noted before, although all children are hurt by the conflict, those who maintain fulfilling relations with both parents do best in the long run. And again, this is where you can really make a difference.

The Silverman family had just ended a custody dispute of two years' duration. Gerald Silverman, father of now eight-year-old Jason, won sole custody of his son. Jason's mother, Loretta, was extremely disappointed and saddened by the outcome of the case. She even contemplated relitigating and suing her lawyer for failing to use a proper strategy. Instead, she held back, went into therapy herself, and began a new life. She saw her son part of every weekend and for one overnight during the week. After initially refusing to talk to her former husband, Loretta began to communicate with him when she realized how Jason was affected by the continuing hostilities.

Loretta and her former husband each became involved with

other people. This helped them to focus more on the future and to dwell less on the unhappiness of the past. Jason adjusted well to living with his father. He relaxed considerably when he knew that his parents were once again speaking to each other and Jason felt comfortable about moving back and forth between homes. Although sad about the divorce, he was doing well in school, had friends, and enjoyed the company of both parents. He knew that his parents would never get back together again; he was just relieved that they were no longer fighting.

□ THE BEST POSSIBLE LIFE □

Although divorce and a custody dispute place tremendous emotional strains on family members, there *is* life after a custody dispute—for parents and for children. What kind of life is largely up to you. You should make every effort to ensure a favorable environment for your child—one in which he can overcome his anxieties and continue his life with confidence. His peace of mind will certainly foster yours.

What factors bode most favorably for a child's future?

1. **The cessation of *all* litigation.**

    It is not enough for *custody* litigation to come to a halt. Any ongoing litigation—even when the issue is finances rather than custody—takes its toll on families. The adversarial system at its worst provides unlimited opportunities for parents to act out their anger at each other and to cause great harm to their children.

2. **An ongoing, fulfilling relationship with both parents.**

    Whatever the outcome of a custody dispute, children will do better in the short and the long run if they can maintain close relationships with both parents. Having one parent identified by an expert and validated by a court decision does not ensure psychological health and peace of mind. Both parents should continue to play an important role in their child's life.

3. **The end of nonlegal hostilities between parents.**

Childen do better if their parents stop fighting. It's as simple as that. If parental hostility dies down, if parents stop putting their children in the middle of some ongoing dispute, their children will be free to get on with the important business of growing up.

4. **New and happy relationships for parents.**

If both parents go on to find happiness in their own lives—ideally, from their work and from new, successful, intimate relationships—they will be better parents and less likely to waste physical and psychic energy on continuing hostilities.

5. **Psychotherapeutic intervention.**

Ideally, all children going through the divorce experience should receive some sort of therapy, even if it is brief. Most do not, which is too bad. Children who have experienced a custody dispute may fare better if they have the chance to develop a warm and nurturing relationship with a therapist. There are no data as yet to support this assertion, but my own experience, and that of many of my colleagues, demonstrates its good sense.

6. **School personnel who are sensitive and understanding.**

Because so many children do go through the divorce experience these days, teachers have become familiar with the effects upon their students. Talk to teachers and to members of the administration at your child's school to learn just how aware they are of this problem. In some schools, support groups for children, led by an experienced counselor or group leader, can help a child express the many complex emotions experienced at this time. Check out what is available in your child's school. Consider establishing some kind of support group yourself if one doesn't exist now.

None of the suggestions presented here guarantees a happy and psychologically intact child following a custody dispute, but these factors can tip the scales in your child's favor and allow you as well as your child to move forward.

Remember always to be child-centered in your choices. In the best of all worlds, this book will have convinced you to abandon litigation and to reach an agreement that can truly protect your children's best interests. But if you have decided to proceed with the litigation, or are even now in the midst of it, you will have the information to do everything you can to protect your children during the process. As you deal with lawyers, judges, psychiatrists, and others, you can make informed decisions.

Psychologists and psychiatrists have their pet theories, lawyers have their professional responsibilities, legislators have their favorite bills, and judges have their preferred presumptions. But none has what you alone possess: the moral, spiritual, and legal right to be responsible for, to take care of, and to love your child. In the name of that right, look deeply within yourself at this most difficult time. And using what you have learned here, remember your child every step of the way.

A P P E N D I X

□ **PROFESSIONAL ORGANIZATIONS** □

American Psychiatric Association
1400 K Street N.W.
Washington, DC 20005
202-682-6000

American Academy of Child and Adolescent Psychiatry
3615 Wisconsin Avenue N.W.
Washington, DC 20016
800-333-7636
202-966-7306

American Academy of Psychiatry and the Law
819 Park Avenue
Baltimore, MD 21201
301-539-0379

American Psychological Association
1200 17th Street N.W.
Washington, DC 20036
202-955-7600

American Bar Association
1800 M Street N.W., Suite 200
Washington, DC 20036
202-331-2200

□ HELP FOR PARENTS AND □ GRANDPARENTS

Committee for Mother & Child Rights, Inc.
Route 1, Box 256A
Clear Brook, VA 22624
703-722-3652

National Organization for Men
381 Park Avenue South
New York, NY 10016
212-686-6253 (MALE)

Grandparents' Children's Rights, Inc.
517-339-8663

National Center for Lesbian Rights (also works with gay fathers)
1370 Mission Street, 4th Floor
San Francisco, CA 94103

Lesbian Mothers National Defense Fund
P.O. Box 21567
Seattle, WA 98111
206-325-2643

Gay and Lesbian Parents Coalition International
P.O. Box 50360
Washington, DC 20004
202-583-8029

□ SCHOOL-BASED SUPPORT GROUPS □ FOR CHILDREN OF DIVORCE

Contact your local school psychologist or social worker. Banana Splits is a concept in children's support groups begun by social worker Elizabeth McGonagle, in Ballston Spa, New York.

◻ **MEDIATION** ◻

American Association for Mediated Divorce
5435 Balboa Boulevard
Encino, CA 91316
818-986-9793

Association of Family and Conciliation Courts
c/o Oregon Health Sciences University
Dept. of Psychiatry
Gaines Hall, Room 149
3181 S.W. Sam Jackson Park Road
Portland, OR 97201
503-279-5651

N O T E S

□ **CHAPTER 1: DIVORCE, CUSTODY,** □
AND THE FAMILY

1. B. A. Weiner, V. A. Simons, and J. L. Cavanaugh, Jr., "The Child Custody Dispute," in D. H. Schetky and E. P. Benedek, eds., *Emerging Issues in Child Psychiatry and the Law* (New York: Brunner/Mazel Publishers, 1985), pp. 59–79.

2. J. W. Jacobs, "Treatment of Divorcing Fathers: Social and Therapeutic Considerations," *American Journal of Psychiatry*, vol. 140 (1983), pp. 1294–99.

3. J. Wallerstein, "Children of Divorce: The Psychological Tasks of the Child," *American Journal of Orthopsychiatry*, vol. 53 (1983), pp. 230–43.

4. W. F. Hodges, *Interventions for Children of Divorce* (New York: John Wiley, 1986).

□ **CHAPTER 2: WHOSE CHILD IS** □
IT, ANYWAY?

1. A. Derdeyn, "Child Custody Contests in Historical Perspective," *American Journal of Psychiatry*, vol. 133 (1976), pp. 1369–76; M. Wyer, S. Gaylord, and E. Grove, "The Legal Context of Child Custody Evaluations," in L. Weithorn, ed., *Psychology and Child Custody De-*

terminations (Lincoln, Nebr.: University of Nebraska Press, 1987), pp. 3–22.

2. In the matter of Baby M, N.J. Supreme Court No. A-39-87, Feb. 3, 1988.

3. S. Goldstein, A. Freud, and A. J. Solnit, *Beyond the Best Interests of the Child* (New York: The Free Press, 1973).

4. See two excellent reviews of joint custody: S. Steinman, "Joint Custody: The Need for Individual Evaluation and Service," in Schetky and Benedek, *Emerging Issues,* pp. 85–99; and A. Tibbits-Kleber et al., "Joint Custody: A Comprehensive Review," *Bulletin of the American Academy of Psychiatry and the Law,* vol. 15 (1987), pp. 27–43.

□   **CHAPTER 3: MEDIATION**   □

1. M. Ruman and M. Lamm, "Mediation: Its Implications for Children and Divorce," in Schetky and Benedek, *Emerging Issues,* pp. 76–84; R. Emery and W. Wyer, "Divorce Mediation," *American Psychologist,* vol. 42 (1987), pp. 472–80.

2. T. Miller and L. Veltkamp, "Disputed Child Custody: Strategies and Issues in Mediation," *Bulletin of the American Academy of Psychiatry and the Law,* vol. 15 (1987), pp. 45–46.

3. S. J. Bahr, "An Evaluation of Court Mediation for Divorce Cases with Children," *Journal of Family Issues,* vol. 4 (1981), pp. 66–79.

4. D. M. Ebel, "Bar Programs: Other Ways to Resolve Disputes," *Litigation,* vol. 6 (1980), pp. 25–28.

5. R. Emery and M. Wyer, "Child Custody Mediation and Litigation: An Experimental Evaluation of the Experience of Parents," *Journal of Consulting and Clinical Psychology,* vol. 55 (1987), pp. 179–86.

6. Carol S. Bruch, "And How Are the Children? The Effects of Ideology and Mediation on Child Custody Law and Children's Well-Being in the United States," *International Journal of Law and the Family,* vol. 2 (1988), pp. 106–26.

7. This comment from personal communication.

□ CHAPTER 8: SOME SPECIAL ISSUES □

1. A. Levy, "Father Custody," in Schetky and Benedek, *Emerging Issues*, pp. 100–114).

2. K. Pruett, *The Nurturing Father* (New York: Warner Books, 1988).

3. D. J. Hutchens and M. J. Kirkpatrick, "Lesbian Mothers/Gay Fathers," in Schetky and Benedek, *Emerging Issues*, pp. 115–26; F. W. Bozett, "Gay Fathers," in F. W. Bozett, ed., *Gay and Lesbian Parents* (New York: Praeger, 1987), pp. 3–22; F. W. Bozett, "Children of Gay Fathers," in Bozett, *Gay and Lesbian Parents*, pp. 39–57.

4. "Custody of Boy Awarded to His Father's Gay Lover," *New York Times*, Nov. 6, 1987, sec. A, p. 14.

5. P. S. Gutis, "Homosexuals Winning Some Custody Cases," *New York Times*, Jan. 21, 1987, sec. C, p. 1.

6. Case citation: S.C. CtAp. 1987 No. 0883 (Feb. 23, 1987), Stroman vs. Williams, as reported in *Family Law Reporter*, vol. 13 (1987), p. 1246.

7. Case citation: In re Birdsall, Calif. CtAp 4th Dist. No. G004357 (Jan. 20, 1988), as reported in *Family Law Reporter*, vol. 14 (1988), p. 1209.

8. Case citation: Miss. CtAp. W. Dist. No. WD 39370 (Dec. 29, 1987), as reported in *Family Law Reporter*, vol. 14 (1988), p. 1131.

9. D. H. Schetky and L. H. Haller, "Parental Kidnapping," *Journal of the American Academy of Child Psychiatry*, vol. 22 (1983), pp. 279–85.

10. G. Dullea, "Stepparents Pressing for Custody Rights as a New Legal Issue," *New York Times*, Mar. 2, 1987, sec. A, p. 1.

□ CHAPTER 11: VISITATION □

1. S. Goldstein and A. J. Solnit, *Divorce and Your Child* (New Haven: Yale University Press, 1984).

□ **CHAPTER 12: RELITIGATION** □

1. F. W. Ilfeld et al., "Does Joint Custody Work? A First Look at Outcome Data of Relitigation," *American Journal of Psychiatry*, vol. 139 (1982), pp. 62–66.

2. P. Ash and M. Guyer, "Relitigation After Contested Custody and Visitation Evaluations," *Bulletin of the American Academy of Psychiatry and the Law*, vol. 14 (1986), pp. 323–30.

I N D E X

abandonment, child's fear of,
    88–89, 222
abduction of child. *See*
    kidnapping of child
acting out and acting in, 14–15
age of child, and reaction to
    divorce and custody
    dispute, 16–23, 80–90
  birth to two, 16
  two to three, 16–17
  four to six, 17, 80–83, 222–24
  seven to nine, 17–18, 83–84,
    89, 222–24
  preteens and teens, 18–20, 85–
    87, 89–90
AIDS, 127
alcoholism, of parent, 138–40
American Association for
    Mediated Divorce
    (AAMD), 47–48
anger, child's feeling of, 14
attorneys. *See* lawyers

Baby M case, 34–35
babysitter, as witness of fact, 104
Banana Splits, 220

"best interest of child" doctrine,
    29–30, 34–37
  "least detrimental alternative"
    principle and, 38–39
  nonbiological parent custody
    and, 36, 145–46
Beyond the Best Interest of the
    Child (Goldstein, Freud,
    and Solnit), 37–39
blame, child and, 14–15
Bruch, Carol S., 55, 56

California, mediation in, 47, 49,
    57
Center for Family in Transition
    (Corte Madera, Calif.),
    44–45
child (children). *See also specific*
    topics
  acting out and acting in by,
    14–15
  age of, and reaction to divorce
    and custody dispute, 16–
    23, 80–90
  birth to two, 16
  two to three, 16–17

child (children) (*cont.*)
  four to six, 17, 80–83, 222–24
  seven to nine, 17–18, 83–84, 89, 222–24
  preteens and teens, 18–20, 85–87, 89–90
  anger of, 14
  "best interest of child" doctrine, 29–30, 34–37, 145–46
  blaming by, 14
  as confidant, 18–19, 87–90
  continuity of relationship with both parents and, 39, 48, 177, 224–26
  the decision and, 163, 171–75
    explaining decision to child, 172–73
    parents' reaction and, 171–72
  denial and, 12–13
  disengagement and, 13
  emotional tasks facing, 12–16
    accepting permanence of divorce, 15
    achieving realistic hope for own future relationships, 16
    acknowledging reality of divorce, 12–13
    disengaging from parental conflicts, 13
    resolving feelings of anger and self-blame, 14–15
    resolving sense of loss, 13–14
  expert witness's meeting with, 117–18

explaining separation to, 62, 63
fear of abandonment, 88–89, 222
feelings of loss, 13–15
forgiveness of parents, 15
guilt feelings, 13, 223
informing of custody dispute, 80–90
  child's taking of sides, 84–88
judge and
  child's desire for contact, 83–84, 89
  meeting *in camera*, 153–55, 160
kidnapping of, 25, 134–38
  children taken abroad, 135
  effect on children, 136–38
  by fathers, 135
  legal issues and, 135–36
  motives for, 134–35
lawyer to represent, 40
"least detrimental alternative" principle and, 38–39
life after custody dispute and, 222–27
as mediator or peacemaker, 44, 69, 85–86
parents' postdivorce relationship and, 173–75, 226
powerlessness of, 14
preparing for trial, 153–55
relitigation and, 198–99, 201–2
resentment of parents toward, 77
school's sensitivity to needs of, 220, 226

taking of sides by, 18–19, 84–88

teacher of, as witness of fact, 100–2

"tender years" presumption and, 32–34

therapy for, 203–20, 226
  child-therapist relationship, 215–19
  choosing a therapist, 210–13, 224
  evaluation by therapist, 208
  group therapy, 219–20
  parents' consultation with therapist, 208–10, 213, 224
  preparing for therapy, 214–15
  symptoms of distress, 203–8
  therapist as witness of fact, 97–100
  trial attended by, 155
  visitation. *See* visitation

child abuse. *See* sexual abuse

child psychiatrist, as expert witness, 107–8

child support, 28–29

co-mediators, 47, 50

conciliation courts, 47

confidant, child as, 18–19, 87–90

co-parenting. *See* joint custody

courtroom, appearance of, 157

cross-examination
  expert witness and, 151
  homosexual parents and, 128–29
  preparing for, 150–51, 156–57

custodial parent. *See also specific topics*
  feelings after decision, 163–67, 170
  visitation and, 28, 39, 181–84 181–84

custody. *See also* custody disputes; joint custody; sole custody; temporary custody

custody disputes. *See also* mediation; relitigation
  alternatives to, 40–42
  historical background of, 31–34
  length of, 25
  reasons for, 26–27
    parents' unconscious needs and fears, 66, 73–78
  resumption of normal life after, 221–27
  telling child about, 80–90
    taking of sides by child and, 84–88

decision, judge's, 162–75
  child and, 163, 171–75
    explaining decision to child, 172–73
    parents' reaction and, 171–72
  living with, 169–71
  losing, 167–71
    depression following, 168
    desire for revenge, 169
    kidnapping of child and, 169
    visitation and, 169, 171
  winning, 163–67, 170
    desire for revenge, 164, 167
    guilt feelings, 164–65

Delaware, mediation in, 47, 49, 57
denial, 12–13
deposition, 92–93
depression, 168
Divorce and Your Child
(Goldstein and Solnit), 177
doctor. *See* physician

economic issues, 11, 28–29
emotional tasks facing the child, 12–16
accepting permanence of divorce, 15
achieving realistic hope for own future relationships, 16
acknowledging reality of divorce, 12–13
disengaging from parental conflicts, 13
resolving feelings of anger and self-blame, 14–15
resolving sense of loss, 13–14
equitable parent, concept of, 145
expert witness(es), 106–21
checking credentials of, 108–11, 113–14, 121
child psychiatrist as, 107–8
court appearance of, 120
court-appointed, 99–100
cross-examination and, 151
lawyer and, 110, 120, 149–51
meeting with child, 117–19
meeting with parents, 114–19
mental health, 151
monitoring of custody arrangement by, 120–21
parent-appointed, 109

payment of, 111
"professional," 110
report of, 114, 116–21
to review opinion of another expert witness, 111–14

fathers. *See also* parents
custody awarded to, 31–33, 123–24
kidnapping of child by, 135
mediation process and, 56
feelings about divorce and custody decision, 11–12
joint custody and, 12
fitness of parents, 32–33
forgiveness, child's, 15
Freud, Anna, 37–39

gay parents. *See* homosexual parents
Goldstein, Sonja, 37–39, 177
grandparents
custody and visitation rights of, 36
taking of sides by, 26, 64–66
group therapy, for child, 219–20
guardian *ad litem,* 40–41
Guardianship of Infants Act, 32
guilt, feelings of
of child, 13, 223
of parent winning custody, 164–65

helplessness, child's feeling of, 14
Hodges, William, 20
holidays, visitation and, 64
homosexual parents, 36, 124–29
AIDS and, 127
cultural disapproval and, 126

female, 125
legal issues and, 126–27
male, 125–26
trial and, 128–29

*Interventions for Children of
Divorce* (Hodges), 20

joint custody, 12, 29, 41–45
child and, 29, 42–45, 67–69
court-ordered, 42–45
drawbacks of, 44
fathers and, 12
important factors in, 43–44
living arrangements and, 29,
42–44, 52–53, 67–69
mediation and, 48
parenting styles and, 43–44,
52, 67
parents' relationship with each
other and, 43–45, 48, 52,
67–69
judge. *See also* decision, judge's
child's desire to contact, 83–
84, 89
child support and, 28
experience of, 59–60
meeting child *in camera,* 153–
55, 160
power of, 27–30
role of, during trial, 159–60
trial delayed by, 148
visitation and, 28

Kentucky, mediation in, 50
kidnapping of child, 25, 134–
38
children taken abroad, 135
effect on children, 136–38
by fathers, 135

legal issues and, 135–36
motives for, 134–35

lawyer(s)
building your case and, 92
choosing, 69–70
courtroom style of, 156
expert witness and, 110, 120,
149–51
fees of, 25
opposing, 156–57
to represent the child, 40
speaking up to, 155–56, 159
trial delayed by, 59, 148
"least detrimental alternative"
principle, 38–39
legal issues. *See also* judge; trial
historical background and,
31–34
homosexual parents and, 126–
27
kidnapping of child and 135–
36
lesbian parents. *See* homosexual
parents
living arrangements
child's adjustment to, 173
joint custody and, 29, 42–44,
52–53, 67–69
loneliness, 66
loss, child's sense of, 13–15

Maine, mediation in, 49–50,
59
Mansfield, Lord, 31–32
Maryland, mediation in, 51
Mead, Margaret, 34
mediation, 25, 46–60
AAMD process, 48
benefits of, 53

mediation (*cont.*)
  children excluded from
      process, 55
  drawbacks of, 55–57
  elements necessary for, 57
  fathers' feelings about, 56
  joint custody and, 48
  Kentucky program, 50
  Maine program, 49–50, 59
  mandatory, 47, 49, 57, 59
  Maryland programs, 51
  mothers' feelings about, 56–57
  questions to ask about, 57–59
  successful, 51–53, 57
  University of Virginia study
      on, 50–51, 56–57
  unsuccessful, 53–55
mediator, 47, 49
  child as, 85–86
  choosing, 57–58
  co-mediator, 47, 50
  qualifications and experience
      of, 49, 58, 59
mentally ill parents, 138–43, 146
  alcoholic, 138–40
  relitigation and, 195–97
  schizophrenic, 141–42
mothers. *See also* parents
  custody awarded to, 11, 31–33
  feelings about divorce and
      custody decision, 11
  mediation process and, 56–57
mourning process, 11, 14

nanny, as witness of fact, 104
nonbiological parents, 36, 143–
  46
  sole custody awarded to, 145–
      46
  visitation and, 144–45

noncustodial parent. *See also*
    specific topics
  child's continuing relationship
      with, 39, 177, 224–26
  depression of, 168
  desire for revenge of, 169

parens patriae, concept of, 31,
  33
parents. *See also specific topics*
  custodial. *See* custodial parent
  equitable, concept of, 145
  fitness of, 32–33
  homosexual, 36, 124–29
    AIDS and, 127
    cross-examination and,
        128–29
    cultural disapproval and,
        126
    female, 125
    legal issues and, 126–27
    male, 125–26
  meeting with expert witness,
      116–19
  mentally ill, 138–43, 146
    alcoholic, 138–40
    relitigation and, 195–97
    schizophrenic, 141–42
  moral and belief systems of,
      36
  nonbiological, 36, 143–46
    sole custody awarded to,
        145–46
    visitation and, 144–45
  postdivorce relationship of,
      173–75, 226
  psychological, concept of,
      38
  rebuilding of lives of, 43, 53,
      68, 69, 226

relitigation and, 199–202
resentment of children by, 77
therapy for, 78
    therapist as witness of fact,
        93–97
unconscious needs and fears
    of, 66, 73–78
physical abuse, 103
physician
    as outside consultant, 104–5
    physical or sexual abuse
        allegations and, 103
    as witness of fact, 102–4
powerlessness, child's feelig of,
    14
psychiatric social workers, 107,
    108
psychiatrists, 107, 110
psychiatry, field of, 151
psychological parent, concept of,
    38
psychologists, 107, 108
psychotherapy. *See* therapy

relitigation, 25–26, 38, 194–
    202
    alternatives to, 202
    child and, 198–99, 201–2
    effect on parents, 199–202
    reasons for, 195–98, 200–1
resentment, toward children, 77
revenge, desire for, 166–69
Ruman, Marilyn and I. Richard,
    47

schizophrenia, of parent, 141–42
school
    sensitivity to child's needs,
        226–27
    support groups at, 220

separation, 61–73
    explaining to child, 62, 63
    living arrangements during,
        70–73
    loneliness during, 66
    sudden, 62–63
    taking charge during, 64–66
    visitation during, 63–64
settlement, after trial begins,
    158
sexual abuse, allegations of, 129–
    34
    after custody dispute, 223–
        24
    false, 131, 132
    interview of child concerning,
        131–33
    physician's statement on, 103
    refuting, 133–34
shared cusatody. *See* joint
        custody
sole custody, 29
    father's seeking of, 123–24
    motivations for, 75
    nonbiological parents and,
        145–46
Solnit, Albert J., 37–39, 177
supervised visitation, 177

Talfourd Act, 32
teacher, as witness of fact, 100–2
temporary custody, 27
"tender years" presumption, 32–
    34
testimony, 159
therapist. *See also* expert witness;
        therapy
    as witness of fact, 97–100
        child's, 97–100
        parent's, 93–97

therapy, for child, 203–20, 226
  child-therapist relationship,
    215–19
  choosing a therapist, 210–13,
    224
  evaluation by therapist, 208
  group therapy, 219–20
  parents' consultation with
    therapist, 208–10, 213,
    224
  preparing for therapy, 214–
    15
  symptoms of distress, 203–8
therapy, for parents, 78
trial, 147–61. *See also* decision,
    judge's; expert witness;
    judge
  child's attendance of, 155
  cross-examination at
    expert witness and, 151
    homosexual parents and,
      128–29
    preparing for, 150–51, 156–
      57
  delays and, 59, 147–49, 158
  dressing for, 158
  feelings after, 160–61
  homosexual parents and, 128–
    29
  judge's role during, 159–60
  length of, 147–49, 158
  preparing child for, 153–55
  preparing yourself for, 155–
    61
  settlement reached during, 158
  testifying at, 159
  typical questions about, 156–
    61

Uniform Child Custody
    Jurisdiction Act of 1968,
    136

Virginia, University of,
    mediation study, 50–51,
    56–57
visitation, 11–12, 176–93
  child and, 178–81, 186–90
    refusal to go, 189–90
    symptoms of illness and
      distress, 186–89
  custodial parent and, 28, 39,
    181–84
  grandparents and, 36
  holidays and, 64
  judge and, 28
  mentally ill parents and, 138–
    43
  nonbiological parents and,
    144–45
  purpose of, 177
  during separation, 63–64
  supervised, 177
  temporary schedule, 27
  trouble points in, 186–93

Wallerstein, Judith, 12, 39
Whitehead, Mary Beth, 34
Wilentz, C. J., 34–35
witnesses. *See* expert witness;
    witness(es) of fact
witness(es) of fact, 92–105
  babysitter or nanny as, 104
  child's therapist as, 97–100
  parent's therapist as, 93–
    97
  pediatrician as, 102–5

ABOUT THE AUTHOR

Stephen P. Herman, M.D., is a child and adolescent psychiatrist and pediatrician. He received his medical training at the Mayo Clinic, the Montefiore Medical Center in New York City, and the Yale Child Study Center. Currently on the faculty at Yale and at the Payne Whitney Clinic, he also taught at both the Albert Einstein and the Cornell Colleges of Medicine. He is a consultant to the New York Supreme Court and Family Court and the Connecticut Superior Courts in custody cases, and is a recognized expert in the medical-legal aspects of child and adolescent psychiatry. He maintains private practices in New York City and Wilton, Connecticut.